791-3401

Soaring with Reading and Writing:
a highly effective emergent literacy program

"The McLaughlin Model"

Josephine McLaughlin & Sylvia Andrews

Trafford Publishing, Inc., Victoria, I

D1511727

© Copyright 2003 Josephine McLaughlin & Sylvia Andrews. All rights reserved.

No part of this publication may be reproduced, stored in a retrieval system, or transmitted, in any form or by any means, electronic, mechanical, photocopying, recording, or otherwise, without the written prior permission of the author.

Printed in Victoria, Canada

National Library of Canada Cataloguing in Publication Data

McLaughlin, Josephine
        Soaring with reading and writing : a highly effective emergent literacy program /
Josephine McLaughlin & Sylvia Andrews.

ISBN 1-4120-0409-8

        I. Andrews, Sylvia II. Title.

LB1525.M234 2003   372.41'6   C2003-902909-3

TRAFFORD

This book was published on-demand in cooperation with Trafford Publishing.
On-demand publishing is a unique process and service of making a book available for retail sale to the public taking advantage of on-demand manufacturing and Internet marketing. On-demand publishing includes promotions, retail sales, manufacturing, order fulfilment, accounting and collecting royalties on behalf of the author.

Suite 6E, 2333 Government St., Victoria, B.C. V8T 4P4, CANADA
Phone   250-383-6864   Toll-free 1-888-232-4444 (Canada & US)
Fax   250-383-6804   E-mail   sales@trafford.com
Web site   www.trafford.com TRAFFORD PUBLISHING IS A DIVISION OF TRAFFORD HOLDINGS LTD.
Trafford Catalogue #03-0778   www.trafford.com/robots/03-0778.html

10   9   8   7   6   5   4

To Patrick, Paul, Nerine, and Gabrielle,
my wonderful, supportive family

J.McL.

In memory of my parents,
Ernest & Elizabeth McAllister,
whose love and example
inspired me to care about others

S.A.

Table of Contents

Acknowledgements

My gratitude and appreciation for all they have done go to the following people:

To my wonderful parents Ralph and Ethel Henry, my sisters Sylvia Green, Ena Henry, and Mignet Broadbelt, and my brother Winston Henry, who have guided me and believed in me all my life.

To Dr. and Mrs. Jiles Kirkland and Oregan Lybass, my dear second family

To Henry Forrester and his wife Hortense, two of my teachers at McIntosh Memorial School, Jamaica, West Indies, who mentored me and encouraged me to further my education; and to my cousin, Millicent Tyndale, who invited me to my first teaching experience in her Pre-School there.

To Ann Killets, Elizabeth Perlman, and Matthew Shoemaker, elementary school principals who first saw that what I was doing in my kindergarten classroom was unique, and who have never stopped believing in what I do. They have encouraged me all the way.

To Wanda Covington, Joanne Hopple, Erika Jones, and Cissy Noland, paraprofessionals who worked alongside me during my years as a classroom teacher. Their cooperation and hard work were invaluable.

To the principals who have welcomed the McLaughlin Model Pilot Program into their schools. Their faith and support have contributed greatly to the success of the program.

To the teachers in the pilot program, who were so willing to open their minds and their classrooms to new methods.

To Louise Grant and the Pew Foundation, who have donated funds for the McLaughlin Model Teacher Training Summer School Program for the past two years.

To the children in the pilot program and the children I have taught: all the boys and girls who entered my classroom over the years. They have brought me much joy and have shown me again and again that my methods work.

To my numerous friends: I have been truly blessed to have them as
my special cheerleaders. They are always there when I need them.

To Dr. Arthur Johnson, Superintendent of Palm Beach County
Schools; Ann Killets, Chief Academic Officer; Dr. Joseph Orr,
(Ret.); Dr. Mary Dupont, Asst. Superintendent of Educational
Equity; Mrs. Gloria Richeson, Area Superintendent, and her very
helpful staff. Without their support and their belief in what I
do, I would not have had the opportunity to establish a pilot
program and share my methods with other teachers.

To all the above who have inspired and supported me, I say,
"Thank you, thank you, thank you!"

Josephine McLaughlin

My appreciation and thanks go to the friends in my writers'
groups, especially Linda Marlow, who gave me valuable feedback on
the chapters in this book.

And my gratitude to my husband, David Andrews, who took the
photographs we used for the cover and inside pages.

Sylvia Andrews

Foreword
by Sylvia Andrews

One February, Josephine McLaughlin invited me into her kindergarten classroom to see how her students wrote. What I saw amazed me. While soft music played, those five and six-year-olds focused and wrote for more than thirty minutes, sounding out words they could not spell. Most of them flowed with writing from one page into the next.

A few more visits during reading time and at other times of the day convinced me that Josephine was the most effective teacher I had met in my thirty years of teaching. What made her success even more remarkable was that many of her students came from low socioeconomic sectors of the community and/or had come into school not speaking English. "You should write a book," I told her. Now, we are writing it together.

Why was I so impressed? Why did what I saw with Josephine's class stand out more than the classes of other excellent teachers that I had visited both overseas and in this country? Let me help you visualize what I found.

Picture a kindergarten classroom where all students believe they are smart, where children learn in small groups at their own pace, and where the energy and excitement you feel around you comes from the students' success and joy in learning.

Imagine a room where children acquire high levels of early literacy skills through meaningful reading and writing, where they become self-disciplined and self-motivated, and where helping others learn and cheering them on to the next step is part of the class spirit.

Can what works so well for one teacher be broken down into steps and strategies that will work for you?

The answer is "Yes". This has been shown by the success

of the teachers and students in the McLaughlin Model Pilot
Program taking place at this time in several schools in Palm
Beach County, Florida

It has been our challenge in writing this book to define
just what makes up the "magic mix" of methods, teacher skills,
and strategies that has been so effective in Josephine's
classroom, and to set it down in writing so that we can pass it
on to you. When you read the chapters that follow, you will
discover the steps you can take to incorporate the McLaughlin
Model into your classroom.

Sylvia Andrews

April 2003

Introduction
by Josephine McLaughlin

I strongly believe that all children who come into regular kindergarten can learn to read and write joyfully and success- fully. I believe that this early success with reading and writing can happen no matter what the socioeconomic status of the students' families, no matter what the students' previous learning experience or the abundance or lack of materials and supplies available to them, and no matter whether or not they come into the class speaking and understanding English.

I have no hesitation in making these statements, because year after year, I watched all the students in my kindergarten classes at a Title One school become readers and writers at least on grade level, but mostly one or two grades ahead of this. Now that I have guided other teachers in the McLaughlin Model Pilot Program and seen their success and excitement, I know that these methods can work for *any* teacher.

We all know that each child learns differently. Children come into school at different developmental stages and with different experiences, so they will learn at their own pace and in different ways. The key to success with this model is that we teachers know where each student is in his or her learning and that we teach all students at the level where they can succeed while being challenged.

In a class of kindergarten students, we might find at the beginning of the year that several come in able to identify all the letters and some sounds, some know perhaps half of the letters, and the rest of the class know no letters or very few letters. When it comes to reading and writing, how could we possibly teach the whole class at the same level? Of course, we couldn't.

One of the key elements of this teaching model is that, shortly after the beginning of the year, we find out the instructional reading level of each student. Then, by the end of the second week, we are able to place them in ability groups so they can learn at their own level. (This small group structure for learning must remain flexible to allow for movement between groups when students show they are ready.)

From that time on, they begin to soar. It is like flying a kite. First you have to provide the impetus to get it airborne (initial success and excitement in learning). Your next challenge is to help it catch the upward momentum (continuing success) and then to keep it going higher by releasing more string (moving into new learning when the student is ready).

How can you provide for each group of students so that learning is not stagnant but moving onward toward the next level? We will show you in this book.

You will find that you are already familiar with some of the methods I use and may already be using some or most of them with your class. The difference with this model is the positive way the methods are used and the way they are combined with cooperative learning. This model of teaching literacy enables the learning process to happen faster and more easily. It enables all children to learn joyfully and at their own pace.

It has given me much pleasure to see that other teachers now using this model are experiencing the same joy and success in teaching that I have felt. Their students are excited about learning and are working cooperatively together to learn. Like me, these teachers are continually amazed at what kindergarten students can achieve.

As my co-author and I wrote this book, we kept in mind that it would be read and used by teachers just beginning the program and perhaps also just starting their teaching careers, so the pace is geared to what we feel a teacher new to the model could accomplish. With my guidance and support, the teachers in the pilot program are working through the steps in this model at a faster pace. It will take time for you to feel secure in moving your students along as fast as they can go. Gradually, you will gain the confidence to do so.

I hope that you enjoy reading this book and that you find much joy and success in using these methods.

Josephine McLaughlin
April 2003

Has the educational community underestimated what kindergarten students can achieve in learning to read and write? We believe this has often been the case.

As you begin this book...

...try to empty your mind of any
preconceptions you may have as to
how much young children can achieve
as they emerge into literacy
and how fast they can achieve it.

Before the Year Begins:
A Look at Guiding Principles

Every school year is a new beginning. Every year we get excited about the children who will soon enter our classrooms for the first time. We know that, in order to achieve success and have a productive year, we have to be ready. Setting up the classroom is just a beginning.

The most important part of being ready is to be mentally prepared. This means taking time to reflect on what we did last year. It means shaking out the principles that have guided our teaching and looking to see if they are taking us in the direction we want to go. It means deciding on any changes we might need to make in these principles.

The more I teach, the more I am convinced that the following principles will lead to success for all teachers:

GUIDING PRINCIPLES

1. Believe in *all* your students, and make sure they know it.
2. Cheer them on to success.
3. Have high expectations.
4. Set your goals and priorities.
5. Use your time wisely.
6. Build a self-disciplined, self-motivated, caring classroom community in which everyone is a teacher and a learner.

1. BELIEVE IN *ALL* YOUR STUDENTS.

I *strongly* believe that every child who comes into my kindergarten class can and will learn. You have to believe this of the children who come into your class, too. It is the greatest gift you can give them. And along with believing in them, it is important to use methods that will lead to success. (You will learn more about these methods in subsequent chapters.)

At the beginning of the school year, you may notice a few students whose work and/or behavior might make you doubt you will succeed with them. Yet, it is important to believe in *all* your students. If you expect less than success, that is what you will get. Year after year, I have watched students overcome considerable difficulties and become successful. The ways I help them are in this book.

Show Students That You Believe in Them.

Make sure you *show* that you believe in every child. You will communicate this with your tone of voice and what you say to each student, and you will do it, whether you realize it or not, with facial expression and other body language. You cannot pretend with body language, so make it a habit to stop and counteract any negative or discouraging thoughts you may have about any student. Say to yourself, "I believe this student will succeed." Notice what each child is doing right and reinforce that. This is one of the keys to having happy, successful students.

> ### *REMEMBER*
>
> Do not prejudge any child as being unlikely to succeed. Children *always* know when you believe in them.

2. CHEER THEM ON TO SUCCESS.

Fig. 0-1-1: "You did so well. Give yourselves a pat on the back."

Some students come into kindergarten already believing in themselves. They are already good listeners, good speakers, and good workers. They have confidence, and they will light the way for other students to follow. We need to help the other students to believe in themselves, too. It is you who can give them the opportunity to do this so that they will not feel less smart, less important, and less talented than the rest. *You* can help build their confidence so that they become successful.

Look for the children who do not participate in discussions, those who do not make friends easily, those who behave in inappropriate ways, and those who look lost because they have never before been in any kind of learning situation. These are the children who already, at this young age, may be experiencing discouragement. Watch constantly for the little steps they take toward success, and cheer them on. Soon you will see them open up and blossom.

How do you cheer your students on to success, especially those students who need their self-esteem boosted? Here are some examples of how I do this. You will find more as you read on through the book.

Ten Ways to Cheer On Your Students

1. From the start of the year, tell your students they are smart and praise them as smart both as a class and as individuals: *"I am so proud of this smart class. You started your work so quickly."*
"Robert knows all these words now. Is he smart or what?"

2. Have the students congratulate themselves. *"You have all finished. Give yourselves a pat on the back and give yourselves a great big hug."*

3. *"I see how quietly Lisa is sitting and listening while Chris teaches her. She knows almost all these letters. Soon she will be one of my teachers."*

4. *"Boys and girls, listen to Manuel read this book. He can read it all by himself."* Afterwards say, *"We are so proud of you, Manuel. Everyone give him a big hand."*

5. *"Look at Andrea's writing! Last week she was only writing one sentence. Now she is writing three. Let's give her a silent cheer."*

6. When a child is about to try something new in front of the class, have the class chant. *"Go, (student's name), go..."*

7. Say, *"I knew you could do it"*... frequently.

8. *"Let's tell Kayla we're proud of her."*

9. *"Look at how well you are walking in line! The whole school knows that you're the best class."*

10. Have the class chant, *"We are smart! We are smart!"* before starting a teaching session.

Figure 0-1-2:

"What a great story! Everyone give him a big hand."

Now you know how to cheer on your young students. Remember to do it often, and don't leave any child out. Yes, cheer *all* your students on to greater success, praise them specifically for what they are doing right, keep them aware of where they are heading, and, by the end of the year, they will amaze you with how much they have learned. This ability to cheer on students is an essential part of success for every teacher.

3. HAVE HIGH EXPECTATIONS

Children will rise to meet whatever expectations we set for them. I know now that, every time I raise my expectations, the students *always* rise to meet them. This happens year after year.

Expect a *lot* from your students, not only in how much they learn but also in how they behave.

Expect your students...

- to focus and listen when you teach and to work quickly and finish work in the given time.
- to respect themselves and each other.
- to respect you and the other adults in your school.
- to follow your class rules.
- to help solve problems in your caring, learning community.

4. SET YOUR GOALS AND PRIORITIES

These days, so much more is expected of teachers than before, and every year the amount of testing and paperwork increases. It is overwhelming at times to all of us. This is why it is more important than ever to get our priorities straight and to have clear goals. I try to give my kindergarten students a well-rounded education, but, no matter what my other goals, my *priority* is to guide students into becoming readers and writers. This will give them the best foundation for the rest of their lives.

My Priority Goals at the Start of Each Year

- to have all students reading and writing independently *at least* at first grade level, with most students reading and writing at higher levels by the end of the year.
- to have reading and writing emerge naturally with no pressure.
- to have some learning and most practice happen through students helping students.
- to have students become self-disciplined, self-directed, and excited about learning.

If you find yourself thinking, "I could never reach those goals", try to shelve your disbelief. Set your goals high anyway, higher than before. Cheer yourself on. Keep telling yourself you can reach your new goals. Try the methods in this book, and you, too, will be amazed at how far your students will go. Then you will *know* that you can do it.

5. USE YOUR TIME WISELY

The school year passes quickly, and before you know it, this year's students will have moved on. It is *very* important to use the time you have effectively. Five-year-old brains absorb knowledge like sponges. Think how much your students have learned in the years before they entered kindergarten: how many words they have learned to speak and how much they have discovered about the world around them. Think about your opportunity to take them from where they are and lead them joyfully as far as they can go along the path of learning.

Some Ways of Using Time Wisely

- It is important that you designate the peak learning time of the day for reading (if possible that first forty-five to sixty minutes in the morning) and it is also important that you incorporate writing every day.

- There are many ways of shortening activities to ensure that learning time is maximized and "busy work" is cut. Be especially careful if you use color, cut, and paste activity sheets, otherwise your students will spend much more time coloring, cutting, and pasting than they do reading and writing. <u>Example:</u> With a "cut and paste" activity sheet on initial consonant sounds, the learning part may be in choosing which pictures begin with "b" and pasting them in place. Coloring the pictures often takes a lot of time… perhaps even fifteen minutes, so I seldom require children to do this. That allows more time to integrate actual reading and writing into this lesson.

7

> Make it a habit to look at each
> activity you ask your class to do
> and reassess its value.

- Train students to guide and supervise group practice... the best way to ensure the daily reinforcing of sight words and letters and the consolidating of many other literacy skills. When students are trained as peer-teachers, you do not need to think of "busy work" as a way to keep them occupied until teacher time is available. They can be actually reading and writing with their peer-teachers.

Harvest the 3 - 5 Minute "Time-Bits"

- Throughout the day, use all the little bits of time you can find that would otherwise be wasted waiting for the bell to ring or waiting for food or… (*You* will know when your "Time-Bits" are) and use these little bits of time for little bits of learning. I use "Time-Bits" to reinforce my sight words, read poems, have students think up sentences around words, say the letters in a particular word, do a simple math word problem, or let one more student share writing or a picture.

Once you get into the habit of doing this, your students become trained. They know when to stop, and they know when to focus. Keep these "Time-Bit" activities light-hearted and fun. Children love the challenge. They become so excited, they don't want to stop.

6. BUILD A SELF-DISCIPLINED, SELF-MOTIVATED, CARING CLASSROOM COMMUNITY IN WHICH EVERYONE IS A TEACHER AND A LEARNER.

In order for students to adjust well to school and be successful, it is important to provide a loving, caring, risk-free environment where they can learn safely and joyfully.

Children come into kindergarten from different home environments. Many of them have never been exposed to a class learning situation before. Some have not been expected to respect the needs of their families and environment or to follow rules. There has to be a common ground. You have to take control and train your students in the behaviors that will lead to a safe, happy, cooperative, and successful learning community.

To promote self-discipline in your students, train them in the expected behaviors and then reinforce in positive ways so that they choose to behave that way. Most children quickly become self-disciplined, but, for a few, it may take most of the year.

You all know how important it is to set boundaries for your students and to clearly communicate these boundaries to them. It is even more important to *consistently* reinforce the boundaries that you set. Consistent reinforcement takes perseverance. Even when your class is behaving the way you want, you will still need to reinforce from time to time so they don't slip back.

> The more self-disciplined your
> students become, the better they will focus
> and learn and so become successful.

Training Students in Responsibility

Within the first few days of the school year, as soon as a few children show they are ready for responsibility, I choose my first student teachers. Then it is my task to model and help these little teachers so that they will be successful. (You will see how I do this in the next chapters.)

It isn't long before other students show they are ready. Then more and more become peer-teachers until everyone has a chance to teach. At this point, the children not only experience excitement at their own success, they share in the success of others.

CONCLUSION

When your guiding principles are in place, so, too, is the foundation and structure for your teaching, and you are all set to take your first step into *The Self-Sustaining Success Cycle.*

The Self-Sustaining Success Cycle

- *Each success makes the students happy and excited...*
- *so they are "turned on" to learning...*
- *so the energy level of the class rises...*
- *so your excitement rises, and you become even more motivated as a teacher to move them on to the next level of learning...*
- *so they experience more success with learning...*
- *so they continue to be happy and excited...*

    ... and so it goes on.

The result of this positive cycle is a classroom of happy, successful, eager, self-disciplined learners.

Phase One

"The First few Weeks"

The Main Literacy Learning Times

1. Group Reading Time (usually at the
    start of the day)
2. Class Literacy Activities Time
    (usually follows Group Reading Time)
3. Center Time: Reading and Writing Centers

The eight Phase One chapters that follow
cover your teaching during the Literacy
Learning Times of the day for the first few
weeks. Though most chapters are introduced
in sequence, they continue together.

Phase 1-1:
Starting on the Right Track

"Welcome to kindergarten. I'm so glad you are here." As the children enter the classroom, I stoop, put my arm around each new student's shoulder, and say, *"I'm so lucky to have you in my class. I know you will love it in this room. You are going to learn so much."*

1. MAKE YOUR STUDENTS FEEL WELCOME

On that first day, after the busy time of parents bringing supplies and after any separation difficulties are over and parents have gone, I gather my students on the rug and welcome them as a class. Most of them are apprehensive and a few are teary-eyed after leaving their parents, so I play some music and encourage them to join me in the actions to a song. We clap hands, touch ears, snap fingers, etc. Then it is time to talk.

2. INTRODUCE CLASS RULES AND BEHAVIOR EXPECTATIONS

"Put your hand up if you have been to Pre-School before," I say. Only a few children do not raise their hands, and I tell the class, *"It doesn't matter if some of you have never been to Pre-School. I am going to make sure that everybody is happy. We will have so much fun in this room. We are just like a family here. I know I have the best boys and girls in my class."*

At this point everyone is quiet and looking at me. *"Did you have rules at pre-school?"* I ask. *"Slip up your hand if you would like to tell us these rules."* We hear a lot of rules: No hitting, no kicking, no biting, no fighting…

Then I continue, pointing to the chart in front of them, *"Well, here are some of the things you have to do to make this class very special."*

1. Do what the teacher tells you to do.
2. Use a quiet voice inside the classroom.
3. Be kind and helpful to others in the class.

I explain each rule in turn, role-playing if needed, and then say, *"I know you are going to remember these rules. Sometimes we forget, so we are going to make sure we remind each other."*

Reinforcing Positive Behavior

Reinforcing positive behavior is the most effective way to achieve your behavior goals, but you need to be specific. For example, when the children get together on the floor the way I want, I say. *"I like the way you moved and sat quietly. Look at the way you are keeping your hands to yourselves. You are not playing with your shoes. You are sitting there waiting for me."* I put my hand on my chest and say, *"I am so impressed. I knew you could do it."* I say this a *hundred* times a day.

If someone is not behaving appropriately, I say with astonishment, *"I don't believe you are doing that, my smart student!"* Then quietly I ask the student, *"Did you forget the rules?"* He nods, and I look at him with confidence. *"I know this won't happen again."* I always finish with a positive statement. My voice tells my students that I really trust them, so they end up feeling good about themselves and wanting to please.

It is also important to affirm students who have broken a rule when you see them start to follow that rule. *"Look at John. Do you remember how he wasn't listening a few minutes ago? Now look at him. He's doing a good job. Stand up, John. Let's give him a big hand."* Then the class says, *"We are so proud of you, John."*

> REMEMBER
>
> It is essential to reinforce your rules.
> Be consistent. You *have* to reinforce the rules
> you set, or your students will not follow them.
> Reinforce your rules *all the time* for the first
> few weeks.

3. THE KEYS TO SUCCESSFUL LEARNING

- Listening and staying focused
- Working quickly and finishing

How do you get five-year-olds to listen, stay focused, and to work quickly and finish? You train them step by step, and you start on the first day of school. This training is important. Take time to do it, and it will pay off a hundred-fold.

Training Students to Listen and Focus

Listening and focusing truly are the most important keys to successful learning. Without my students being able to listen and focus well, it would be impossible for them to achieve so much by the end of the school year. They have to be taught how to do this. They have to be taught the behaviors that will lead to success.

- During the first few days, begin to teach these skills in a gentle, positive way. Don't assume that they will know what to do when you say "Listen" or "Focus". Talk to the students about what a good listener does and what a poor listener does, and then show them. Role-play both good listening and poor listening so that the students can differentiate between them and learn to listen well. For most students, the habits of focusing and listening will form quickly, but for some, it can be a slow process.

- Keep in mind that prolonged activities, whether it be Circle Time or seatwork or group discussions, can contribute to inattention. Begin the year with short activities and gradually extend them as student listening habits improve.

- Instead of continuing to teach when a student is not listening and focusing, stop and wait for them to attend. Taking the time and having the persistence to do this early in the year, pays off in saved time later. When they are all focused, you get to teach and your students get to learn.

- When it is time for the students to come up to the front, sit on the floor and listen, train them to do this in a way that will have them quiet and ready to listen.
  "Table One, stand. Push your chairs in, and sit on the floor quietly," I say. Then I turn to the rest of the class, *"Look at the way they walked to the floor. Look how quietly they are waiting. I am so impressed!"* I call Table Two.

- Once they are all sitting, I take my seat in front of them and say, *"I'm ready... and I'm waiting."* And I wait as long as it takes. It doesn't take long because my eyes are roving and wherever behavior is inappropriate, I look steadily at that student. Very slowly the silence speaks. Then I say, *"Thank you (student's name), for looking at me and listening. Now we are ready to begin."*

Training Students to Work Quickly and Finish:

First Seatwork Activity

As you reinforce good listening and staying focused, keep activities short and simple. To train all my students to work quickly and complete their work, this is what I do:

- I hand each child a sheet of paper with an apple shape drawn on it and say, *"Take out your red crayon. Hold it up. Look around and make sure the person next to you is holding a red crayon. Now, color your apple red."*

- As I walk around, I notice a few students struggling. I take an apple shape and say, *"Let me show you how you can finish*

coloring your apple in no time. Watch me color my apple.
I am making long strokes. Am I doing a good job?"

"Yes," comes the response.

"Look, I'm all done. Now you go ahead and finish your apple.
I know you can do it." This modeling does the trick. Before
long, everybody is trying the long strokes.

Fig. 1-1-1:
Everybody tries
coloring with
long strokes.

- *"Now, get your green crayon. Color the leaves green."*
  I cheer them on to finish: *"Keep working. You are doing a*
  good job. You are such fast workers."

- I walk around again and notice that Willy, who had said he
  couldn't do it, is now almost finished. *"Look at that! You did*
  a great job. I'm so glad to see you try."

- When they *all* have finished, I call on the children at each
  table to stand in front of the class and display their apples.
  Then I acknowledge everyone's effort, and tell the children that

I love each apple just the way it is.

> It is important to be accepting and happy with what your young students produce. They will know if you don't like their efforts, and this will discourage them from trying and taking risks in learning.

When they finish showing their work, I tell them, *"I'm so proud that everyone has finished. Now we can move on to another activity."*

4. FIRST READING: SIGHT WORDS

Introduce the children to reading sight words from the first day of school. Keep a pile of 3" x 4" cards handy for this purpose and add several words a day. You will be amazed at the number of words these five-year-olds can learn to read in just the first few weeks as long as they have daily reinforcement.

- On this first day, try the following activity. Say, *"All the boys stand on this side of the room and all the girls stand on the other side."* Show them the word 'boys' and the word 'girls' by writing them on the chalkboard. Have them say the letters in each word.

- Now begin a movement activity where they walk around the room. Tell all the girls to jump, then all the boys.

- Write the word 'jump' on a card and say, *"Let's say the letters in the word 'jump'."* (It is important to get the students to say the letters in <u>all</u> the flash card words they learn. This makes them look carefully at the words and also reinforces recognition of lowercase letters.)

- Next make two cards, one with 'girls jump' and one with 'boys jump'. Tell the class, *"We're going to play a fun game,"* Show them the new cards, and read the words aloud together. *"When I show you these cards, you have to remember to do what they say."*

Then play the "girls jump/boys jump" game for a few minutes.

> This game on the first day of school helps students to feel that school is fun. They are combining learning with large movements, one of the best ways for young children to learn.

5. FIRST WRITING

Learning to write the letters of the alphabet also begins on the first day of school. After lunch, I tell the students to take out their "Welcome Apple" picture that they have colored.

- *"Now we are going to write the word "apple" underneath the picture. Watch me write the 'a'."* I model drawing the circle and ending with the stick, then ask for two volunteers to write it on the board. As they write, I remind them to draw the circle to the left and to draw the stick from top to bottom. *"Now everyone, write the "a" under your apple."*

- My assistant and I walk around showing them where to start writing and cheering them on. It is not unusual for some students to tell me they can't do it. *"Keep saying "I can" until you finish."* I tell them. Again I encourage them to work quickly. This is a habit they need to acquire.

- I model each letter, and they write as my assistant and I move around cheering them on to finish, just as we did with the "a". Soon they have written the word "apple".

- Once more I get the children at each table to stand and display their work. Everybody cheers for the groups as they take turns to stand. No matter what the writing looks like, I tell them I love what they did and how they tried so hard and worked so quickly.

19

CONCLUSION

Soon all my students are in the habit of finishing their work quickly. Soon they know that I will not teach until *everyone* is listening and focusing. They know that whenever someone is showing inappropriate behavior, I will simply stop and wait.

> Speak positively to your students, believe in them, and train them in the habits that will lead to success.

**Your first day is over.
What comes next?**

Within the next three to four days:

- You will introduce letter learning, which will continue for a while.

- You will begin training peer-teachers.

- You will assess to find what letters each student recognizes.

- You will continue introducing new sight words and reinforcing these words daily. This will be ongoing until most groups are reading books.

- You will begin your nursery rhyme charts (See Phase 1-6)

- And you will start your Reading and Writing Centers. (Phase 1-8)

The first four activities are covered in the next two chapters. They will lay the foundation for starting ability reading groups, which will form during the second week.

```
┌─────────────────────────────────────────────────┐
│          ┌─────────────────────────┐             │
│          │      Phase 1-2:         │             │
│       ┌──┴─────────────────────────┴──┐          │
│       │    Learning the Letters       │          │
│    ┌──┴───────────────────────────────┴──┐       │
│    │ & Training Students as Peer Teachers │       │
│    └──────────────────────────────────────┘       │
└─────────────────────────────────────────────────┘
```

It is truly amazing to see how quickly kindergarten students can learn to recognize the upper and lowercase letters when they are free from pressure and they do it themselves. This process, along with learning to recognize whole words by sight, will lead the class right into reading. While introducing learning the letters and starting sight word recognition, I also begin training students to be peer-teachers. This chapter includes the following:

- Finding out which letters your students know.
- Steps for introducing peer-teaching.
- Reinforcing the letter learning and promoting cooperative learning.
- Checking on the letter learning.
- Recognizing lowercase letters.
- Using movement to assist learning.

1. FINDING OUT WHICH LETTERS YOUR STUDENTS KNOW

Children enter kindergarten with different prior experience. Some have attended pre-school or have received teaching at home. However, there are always some for whom the classroom situation is new, some who do not know the letters or even how to hold a crayon. With the students' diverse experience in mind, I start the year by giving a quick, informal assessment that will show me which letters each child knows.

First, I write the uppercase letters of the alphabet in random order on a chart and post it in front of the class. Then I write the letters randomly on a sheet of paper and copy this for each child. (If you feel strongly about writing both uppercase and lowercase letters together on the chart and individual sheet, that's okay, too.)

"These are the A, B, C's," I tell the students with excitement in my voice, pointing to the chart. *"How many of you smart boys and girls know them?"* Many students raise their hands.

"I have the same letters on this sheet of paper for each of you. Later in the week, I will call you up to see how many letters you know. Every time you name a letter correctly, I will circle it and put a smiley face there."

Within the next few days I assess all the students. They become so excited with the smiley faces that they are anxious to learn to name more letters so that their sheet can be filled with smiles.

To make this experience fun for the students, they need to understand that it is okay to know all the letters, and it is also okay not to know any. *"Don't feel sad if you don't know the letters now, because we're all going to learn them together,"* I tell them.

I encourage the children to help each other learn the letters, and I give positive reinforcement when I see them doing this.

Why Start with Uppercase Letters?

It is much easier for these young children to recognize the uppercase letters. The lowercase letters are more complex to learn because several of them ("b" and "d" or "p" and "q") look so similar that students can become confused and have difficulty achieving success.

<u>How and when do the students learn lowercase letters?</u>

It is not that we have left the lowercase letters for later; we are learning them as we go along. We point them out daily on flashcards, in poems, etc., when we say the letters of the words. (See Section 5 at the end of this chapter.)

2. STEPS FOR INTRODUCING PEER-TEACHING

It is always possible to find a few children who know all the letters of the alphabet. Once you identify these students, you can begin the training.

- First, model the left to right sweep across the chart.
- Next, choose one student to point to the letters on the chart while the others name the letters. When the naming of all the letters is completed, praise the student who pointed, *"Give him a big hand. He did a super job, and everyone paid attention so well! Later someone else can try."*

Fig. 1-2-1:

Paraprofessional guides a peer-teacher as he leads a group practice for the first time.

- The next day, divide your class into two groups. Choose two students who can recognize all the letters to take over the two groups. One group will name the letters on the chart. The other will work with flashcards.

While one group works with the letter chart, you can model the use of letter flashcards for the second group. As the students name the letters, place them face down on top of each other on the floor until all the cards are gone. Next, ask the selected student to flash the cards. When the student finishes, don't forget to praise him or her. *"Great job! You held the cards so that everyone could see."*

- For the next few days, allow these two groups to work for at least ten minutes every morning. Continually affirm students who are being attentive. *"Look at Alicia. She is sitting so nicely and saying the letters. She is not crawling around. She is sitting just like a first-grader. I know she will soon be one of my teachers."*

Fig. 1-2-2:

A peer-teacher independently leads a small group in letter recognition practice.

As you can imagine, all the students want to be praised, so they try to do their best.

There are always a few children who will have difficulty attending no matter what time of the year or how great the motivation.

I quietly take these few students aside before they affect the others. My assistant and I will work with them until they are able to join the others. These are students who will need modifications in my approach and also extra positive reinforcement. I teach them little strategies with certain letters to help them remember, so that they become successful.

Jason rushes to me with excitement in his face and says, "Mrs. McLaughlin, Cory knows a lot of letters now." Back in his group, Cory's face lights up. I hurry over.

"Cory, I am so excited that you have learned the letters! Let me hear you say them." Cory points to the letters he knows and says them.

"You did a great job," I tell him. _"I am so proud of you both."_

3. REINFORCING THE LEARNING AND PROMOTING COOPERATIVE LEARNING

Each time the whole class gathers, I have the students "show what they know":

"Let me see the hands of all those who have smiley faces on their sheet." As the hands go up, I affirm them. *"Give yourself a pat on the back and give yourself a great big hug. This is such a smart class. You just came to kindergarten, and you already know so many letters."*

Then I ask for volunteers to point to the letters and say them. The class sits quietly as Josh points and says the letters. *"Super job, Josh! Let's give him a big hand."* His face lights up as they cheer for him. *"Tell Josh he is a smart boy,"* I say. They all respond. Now more students want to show what they know.

Andre, who has never been to pre-school, slips up his hand. "Mrs. McLaughlin, can I say the letters?" He walks to the chart, points to two letters and names them.

"I'm so proud of you, Andre. Soon you will be able to say all the letters. Boys and girls, who will help Andre to learn more letters?"

"I will!" "I will!" come the responses.

Everyone wants to help Andre. I choose a student to work with him at Quiet Time. Other students also get help from their classmates at this time. I provide a set of note cards with the alphabet for each peer-teacher. They are responsible for keeping these cards in a safe place. During Quiet Time they take their partners by the hand and find a place to work.

4. CHECKING UP ON THE LEARNING

I check the students regularly on separate letter assessment sheets (opposite) so I can see how each is progressing.

Alphabet Recognition

Circle the letters when students name them.

Student's Name _____ Date completed _____

H   Y   C   M   Q   I

E   W   T   X   Z   L

V   P   A   G   R   S

U   D   K   N   O   J

F   B

> *"Look at all the letters you named, Jennie. I can't believe it!"* I say with excitement. *"As soon as you can name some more letters, let me know so that I can put more smiley faces on your sheet. Soon you will be one of my teachers. You are doing a super job."*

After just a few weeks, most of the students know all the letters. Of course, a few students will take longer, and I let them have whatever time it takes.

> It is important to realize that while this letter learning is going on, the students are mastering *many* sight words.
>
> Even students who are having difficulty with isolated letters at this point are able to recognize some sight words. Yes, students can recognize a seemingly more complex series of letters when they cannot yet recognize isolated letters. How can this be? It is because words have meaning.
>
> When you introduce a sight word, make it come alive for students by using it in a sentence, acting it out, and discussing the students' experiences with the word. Putting sight words into context seems to make all the difference. It gives meaning to the words. This is why we should not wait to start children reading until after they know the letters.

5. RECOGNIZING LOWERCASE LETTERS

Lowercase letters are everywhere in my classroom. They are on the flashcards, in the poems hung on the walls, on the news and interest charts, on the chalkboard, and on the word lists and sentence strips in the Reading Center.

The students learn these letters incidentally during the work we do each day, because I constantly ask students to point to specific words and say the letters in them to the class. (They quickly learn this is called "spelling the words".) This simple activity, done frequently, not only teaches them to recognize the lowercase letters, but helps them begin to learn to spell the words they will want to write. What better way to reinforce letter recognition?

6. USING MOVEMENT TO ASSIST LEARNING

Young children learn best when they are allowed to touch, to manipulate, and to actively participate. That is why, when they are learning to recognize the letters of the alphabet, it is important to give your class opportunities to move around and have fun. They can also sit down and cut and match letters, but best of all, they love the movement activities.

Three of their favorite movement activities are "Musical Letters", "Pick Two", and "Find Your Partner".

"Musical Letters"

1. In random order, place uppercase and lowercase letter flashcards on the floor in a big circle. Students stand in the circle beside the cards.
2. When the music starts, they march around. They pick up the card closest to them when the music stops.
3. Next they find the person with the matching uppercase or lowercase letter and stand with them.
4. Call on several students to name their letters.

5. The children then place the letters back on the floor ready for the next round. Start the music, and the game continues.

"Pick Two"

1. Bring the class up to sit in front of the chalkboard.
2. Post magnetized uppercase letters randomly on the board and place lowercase letters in a box.
3. Divide the class into two teams.
4. One student from each team picks two letters from the box and places them under their matching uppercase letters.
5. As soon as each student returns to the group, the next student goes up to choose two more letters.
6. The game is over when all the letters are matched.

"Find Your Partner"

1. Tape upper and lowercase letters to the chests of students.
2. When the music stops, they look for the person with the matching letter and stand with them.
3. Students then say the letter and sit down. The goal is to have everyone matched before the music starts again.

CONCLUSION

By making it a habit for students to say the lowercase letters in the sight words they learn and making the learning risk-free and fun, you will find that almost all the students quickly master the skill of identifying the letters. By training students to be peer-teachers, you are causing much more learning to go on in the classroom while teaching responsibility. You have set up an ideal teaching-learning situation.

Phase 1-3:
Beginning to Read with Sight Words

1. CHOOSING THE WORDS

As you have seen in "Starting on the Right Track", you can introduce your students to sight words from the first day of school. How do you choose which words to use?

Choose ...

... words that are meaningful to the students in their lives at home and at school, for these are the words they will want to write,

... words they will meet frequently in the first books they read in class,

... words they will meet in the poem charts and other wall charts,

... and everyday words that crop up spontaneously during the routine activities of school.

It is important to note that once the children are reading books in their groups, there is no longer a need to accumulate flashcards of new words. However, we will continue to add words to the Word Wall throughout the year. Students will reinforce the new words they meet by seeing them and saying them over and over as they read each book with their group. It is a good idea, however, to use flashcards when working with the easily confused 'wh' and 'th' words and some other families of words like someone, somebody, everyone, everybody, etc.

At the end of this chapter is a list of sight words that I commonly introduce at this beginning phase. However, every teacher's list will vary according to the books or stories the children will read first and the words they want to use from their lives.

> Learning to read sight words is an ideal way to get your students feeling excited about learning and confident about moving ahead into reading. Children can experience success in reading much more quickly through starting with reading sight words than through beginning with letters and their sounds in a phonics approach to reading. Learning phonics, however, is an important part of a successful approach to young students becoming readers and writers, so I begin teaching letter-sounds in Phase 1-7 within the first few weeks of school.
>
> Learning to read sight words also provides students with further opportunities to work cooperatively to help each other learn.

2.   INTRODUCING THE SIGHT WORDS

In the first chapter of Phase One, "Starting on the Right Track", I explained one way to introduce the first sight words of the year. Here is another way of introducing sight words, one that will encourage your students to look closely and notice small differences between words.

- When the children have gathered in the front, I say with excitement, *"I have a new word for you. It is the word 'see'. Let me write it. Now, let's say the letters together."*

- After we spell 'see', I ask. *"What do we use to see things?"* They tell me we see with our eyes. *"Look around the room and name some things you can see."* They name things around the room.

  "Boys and girls," I say, *"there is another word called 'sea'. It is the sea that you swim in. Watch me take away one of the e's in 'see' and put an 'a' there. Now look! We have a new word."*

- We spend a few minutes having fun by substituting the "a" for the "e" and back again and having the students tell me which "see" or "sea" it is. Then I move to the word "fish".

    "Who knows what lives in the sea?"

    They tell me, "fish". I write the word 'fish' on a card. *"This is the word 'fish',"* I tell them. *"Spell the word 'fish'."*

    "Now, let's pretend to swim like a fish," I say. We all swim around the classroom.

- At this point I start my word chart by writing the new words on it. I want the children to see these words at all times, and having the words displayed on a word chart gives me the chance, any time in the day, to stop and review them.

> On an average I introduce about five new words every day. Many of the children quickly learn these words because they are taught in a meaningful way and are reinforced daily.

Sometimes a word comes spontaneously from a discussion or a routine classroom situation. For example, if I say, *"Now, walk to the door"*, I could teach the words "to" and "walk". For most of the students it seems to take just that initial introduction to a word for them to remember it.

This constant adding of words to the class word chart and to the flash cards packs they are accumulating enables students to learn to recognize many new words in just a few weeks.

3. REINFORCING WORD RECOGNITION

Being able to quickly recognize these initial sight words is very important. We practice them several times a day for the first few weeks. Discovering they can recognize words builds confidence and encourages students to be willing to venture further into reading.

As well as having the sight words on the word chart, one set of sight word flash cards is always waiting where we gather on the rug as a whole group. Another set is in the Reading Center.

These daily sight word practices serve three purposes:

- to reinforce the words.
- to focus the class before I begin to teach a new lesson.
- to give practice in cooperative learning with peer teachers.

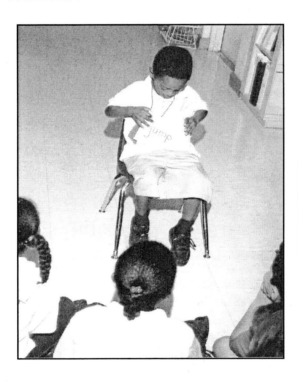

Fig. 1-3-1: Peer-teacher leads a flashcard practice session.

4. PLAYING "WORD DETECTIVES"

After introducing some words, it is time to stimulate the students' thinking by using further strategies to get them to look more closely at each word.

"Look at every word," I say to them, *"You never know when you may find a little word hiding inside a bigger word."*

I write the word "your" on the board and say, *"This is the word 'your'."* I pick up a backpack and say, *"This is your backpack"* to a student. *"Now, let me cover up the 'r' in 'your'. What word do you see?"* Lots of hands go up to tell me they see the word "you".

Then I write "can't" on the board and say, *"If you cover up the 't, you'll get a word."*

"Can," they tell me. It is one of our favorite words. Together we look at the words "them" and "sat" to find the little words inside the big ones.

I introduce this "words inside a word" concept during the first month of school and soon find that students stop me when we are reading poems or the weekly newspaper, etc., to show me how they can cover up part of a word and have another little word. When this happens, I use both words in sentences right away so they can differentiate between the meanings.

This activity encourages children to look closely at words, so take time for them to do this during poetry reading or Big Book reading. Always be willing to stop to let a student point out the little word inside a bigger word. Spending quality time on this skill catches their interest and encourages them to focus on print.

When children take part in this fine focus on words, it seems to turn on a switch in their brains. This is especially so with students taking tiny steps. What a difference this can make to those students! It enables them to learn.

5. STARTING A WORD WALL

You can begin the class Word Wall during the first two weeks of the year. The goal is to make it attractive and to have the word cards a size that the children can comfortably use. Do not place in alphabetical order at the beginning.

- Randomly place the sight words at the bottom of the Word Wall where they are accessible to the students.

- Add high frequency words constantly: words they use in their writing and words from the reading they do from the poem charts.
- Add words you use when you model writing.
- A few weeks into the year have your class help you put the words in alphabetical order. Remove a few words at a time. Have the students name the words and tell you which letter of the alphabet they go under. Then pin or staple the words under the appropriate letter heading.
- Use your Word Wall often. Use it during the last part of the day or when you are transitioning between activities. Have a student name all the words under a specific letter or decide on words that you would like to add onto a letter that only has a few words.

The more you use the Word Wall, the more familiar the students are with the words on the wall. When they know the words, they will be able to find them when they want to use them in writing.

The Next Step

When learning the letters is under-way, and the word chart has accumulated 15 - 20 sight words, it is time to get Reading Group Time started and time to choose the students who are ready to be challenged. You will learn how to do this in the next chapter.

6. WRITING WORD LISTS AT HOME

I also encourage students to write as many of the sight words as they can remember on a sheet of paper at home and bring it in to me. Most students love to do this. I get excited when students hand me their little lists, and make sure to have them come up at Circle Time to show their work and read the words to the class. Then I post the lists so that other students are encouraged to do this reading-writing activity.

Figure 1-3-2:
This is a list of words written from memory by a student. By seeing sight words often, students can write some of them correctly without the effort to learn spelling.

7. SCRAMBLED WORDS

Once the students have learned quite a few sight words, I waste no time before challenging them with the fun activity of "Scrambled Words". I mix up the magnetic letters for the word "can" and place them on the board. *"These letters make up one of the words you know, but the letters are all mixed up,"* I tell them. *"I know how smart you guys are. I bet you can guess what word this is. I could never trick you."* They look at the letters and in a flash several hands shoot up.

I choose a student to come up and unscramble the letters. *"I knew you could do it,"* I tell him. I put up some more mixed-up words. Very quickly most of the students get the idea. The rest will soon learn. They love the challenge of solving the puzzle.

At first I use magnetic letters, but later on, when we want more practice with fine motor skills, they have to come up and write the letters in the correct order. "Scrambled Words" continues all year with the students becoming more skilled at unscrambling.

This activity helps to improve their reading and writing, as it reinforces their visual memory of the words and helps them to spell the words they want to write. You can use this, even with "tiny step" students, to reinforce some of their vocabulary words when they are reading books.

8. FLASHCARD GAMES

Just as my students play alphabet games with music, they also play games with the word cards.

Here are two games I use:

"Pass the Flashcards"

1. Have students sit in a circle. Distribute the sight word flashcards. Once the music starts, they pass their cards around to the right.

2. When the music stops, call on the children, one at a time, to name their words. If a child doesn't know the word, he or she says the letters and other students can name the word.

3. An extension to this activity is to stop the music and ask a student to use his or her word in a sentence.

"Beanbag Word Toss"

1. First, write the sight words on a plain, brightly-colored twin bed sheet. (The alternative is to spread a few flashcards on the sheet.) It is important to start with just a few words, so that the students will not get confused. Then keep adding more as you introduce new words. Remember to leave good space between each word.

2. Students sit around the sheet. Give a beanbag to any student, who will toss it so that it lands on a word. Allow three chances to land on a word. The student names any word the beanbag lands on and, if correct, spells the word and uses it in a sentence.

9. CHECKING UP ON THE LEARNING

It is easy to check up on how many of the sight words your students can recognize. Just write or type the words on a sheet of paper, make one copy per student, and have the students read through the words they know for you to check or circle. Test each student again every two weeks, and keep the dated total of words read correctly on each sheet for your records. An example of an early sight word checklist is on the next page.

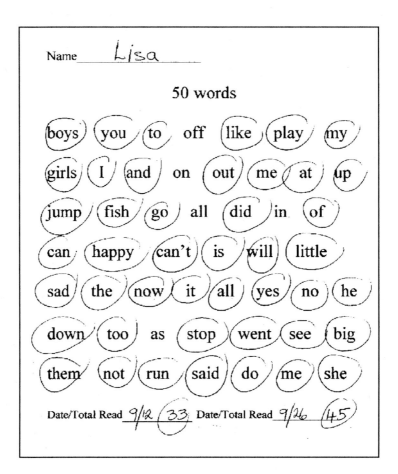

8. KEEPING THE LEARNING AND MOTIVATION FLOWING

Some students learn these initial sight words so quickly that I know I must think of other materials and activities to challenge them and keep their level of excitement flowing. This is why I introduce poem charts right from the start and follow these with the weekly children's newspaper and other teacher-made charts so that they can find the words they know in context and learn others incidentally.

By using additional materials and activities, you will ensure that your students are always able to keep progressing and making great strides as readers. (I will explain more about using these supplementary materials and other ways of reading sight words in context in Phase 1-6).

As you saw on page 38, once I have identified the more advanced students, I form ability reading groups. From the work we do with nursery rhymes and the work we will do in the next three chapters, they will already know how to read left to right and will also be able to identify many sight words by the time they read their first book. You, too, will quickly identify the students in your class that are fast learners. Then you will need to provide experiences to keep their brains stimulated.

REMEMBER

The worst thing a teacher can do to self-motivated students is to allow them to stagnate. That is when boredom sets in, and bored students can become behavior problems. This can happen to even the best students. You have to know your students and know when to move them on to keep the level of excitement flowing.

CONCLUSION

Every year, as I watch all but a few of my students reading these basic sight words within a few weeks and see the joy in their faces and their eagerness for learning, I feel exhilarated. Their success reinforces my belief that children can reach the expectations you set for them if you provide a positive and joyful learning environment.

(A list of beginning Sight Words is on next page.)

Here are *some* of the basic sight words that I use: (not in order of use)

I   you   your   boys   girls   big   little   my   me   we
like   love   apple   happy   sad   in   out   and   but
are   book   do   did   up   down   stop   go   went
house   home   sit   jump   walk   run   ride   play
sea   see   to   can   can't   say   look   the   they
fish   it   is   day   on   sun   funny   bus   have   of
off   class   school   pool   teacher   he   she
Mom   Dad   brother   sister   friend

(I also begin teaching the color words and number words early in the year.)

┌───┐
│ ┌───────────────────────┐   │
│ │ Phase 1-4:   │   │
│ ├───┐   │
│ │ Starting the Reading Groups   │   │
│ └───┘   │
└───┘

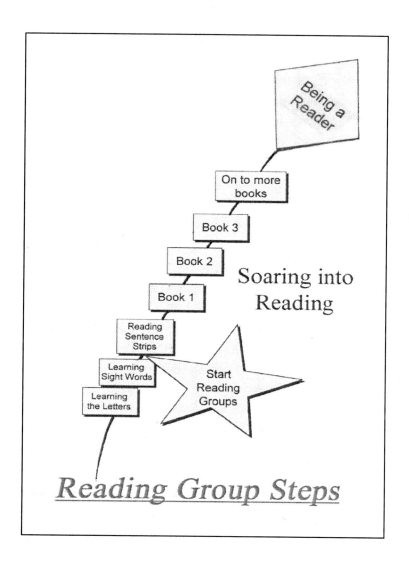

Now that we are in the second week of school, it is time to begin to form the reading groups. My goal is to have students working in ability reading groups almost from the start of the year, so I begin this process early.

What has happened so far with groups?

During the previous two chapters, the students have already begun working in randomly chosen groups led by peer teachers as they build their letter recognition and sight word skills. They are able to remain in these groups and focus for about ten minutes or more.

As you work with the groups and move them into the next steps, you will find that their ten minutes focus time will gradually increase until it becomes twenty, then thirty, and finally forty-five minutes. Take time to stop at each group to observe, assist, and cheer them on to success. The training you give them and your expectations will help your students to focus longer. Watch your students and notice when they start to get restless. When that happens, it is a signal to end Reading Group Time for the day.

BEGINNING TO FORM ABILITY READING GROUPS

Finding the students who are ready to move on

Randomly chosen groups led by peer teachers are working with the Letter Chart, with letter flashcards, with sight words at the Sight Word Chart, and with sight word flash cards. Since the second day of school, I have been assessing each student's letter recognition. It is now time for me to find those students who can recognize all or most letters and who have quickly mastered most of the sight words the class has learned so far (15 - 20 words). These are the students who are ready to be challenged and who need to move on.

Forming the Top Group

Once I identify the students who are doing well with the letters and sight words, I bring them together as a group in front of the Sight Word Chart. There I remind them how to work cooperatively, taking turns to point and read down the columns of words. If they don't know a word, they know the others can help them. After watching the first two students point and read, I leave them and go to check up on the other groups.

> Picture yourself moving around the four groups encouraging them to focus, affirming their efforts, reminding them to take turns, and stopping to call on a particular student to say the letters or the words. Remember, the peer teachers are managing the groups. *"I'm watching for the students who are looking at the letters and saying them. I'm looking for my next teachers,"* I tell them.

When I come back to the top group at the word chart, I praise them for the way they have worked so well together and taken turns. Then, I listen to them read the words and confirm that almost all are ready to move on to sentence strips. A few will need to spend a day or two more on reinforcing the words on the chart. They will lead the group of students that moves up to work at the Sight Word Chart during Group Reading Time.

"You are doing so well," I tell the group. *"Tomorrow some of you will learn how to read sentences,"*

The Sentence Strip Group

This is how to move the top group into reading sentence strips in the pocket chart:

- Write sentences on strips. These sentences are made up of words they already know and a few new words. Then put the sentence strips in a pocket chart.

- The next day at Group Reading Time, rearrange the groups. 1/ Move the top group to the "Sight Word Sentence" pocket chart.

47

2/ Move the children who know 15 - 20 letters and can identify some of the sight words to the Sight Word Chart to be led by the students remaining there. As they learn the sight words and spell the letters in them, their letter recognition will improve.

3/ Now that the two letter learning groups are smaller, combine them into one group. The students left with the letters will continue working at learning them for a while. Try to spend quality time with them, as you want them to be successful, and remember to keep working with them on learning sight words.

Introducing Reading Sentence Strips

After settling the other groups, stay with the Sentence Strip Group and read each sentence to the students, pointing out new words. (See Phase 1-5 for how I work with new words in the sentences.) These new words will be added to the Word Wall.

Begin this activity with four sentences and add new sentences in a day or two. The main purpose for this sentence strip step is to have the students see the sight words in context and to reinforce pointing and reading in a left to right sweep. From the beginning of the year, with the whole class, model the "pointing and reading left to right" skill every time you read the rhymes and poems on charts along with your class.

What is very important during the time this group works at reading sentences is that you look at the first books the students will be moving into and gradually include almost all of the words in the sentences. That way, by the time they start reading their first book, there will only be one or two words that they don't know.

This three group structure only remains the same for one or two days because you need to observe the group working independently at the list of sight words to tell you which students are ready to move on to sentence strips for their next challenge. Don't be surprised that you are already thinking of moving students on from this group. Moving students on to the next step is what this literacy model is all about. From the moment your students are ready and start moving on to the next challenge, they begin to soar.

Group Reading Time should happen as early in the day as possible. When the students come in, they are fresh and can focus better. In a matter of a month or so, the children will know exactly where they have to go when Group Reading Time begins.

Every day they see the material, they read, and, when they are ready, they move ahead. This is an essential part of what makes group reading work. Reading becomes a routine part of the day. You are not just pulling one group to listen to them read. All the groups read every day, and you are able to spend time with each group.

CONCLUSION

Group Reading Time is the main ingredient in the "soaring" that begins to take place. These groups provide the structure that enables students to work and learn at their own pace. It is the ability to move on when you are ready that fuels the excitement and the energy for becoming a reader. Reading Group Time should take place every day. It is too important to skip.

However, group reading is just one part of your daily Literacy Time. Once the group reading is over each day, you move into working as a class with the other literacy skills the students have to master. That is the time when you work through the steps of teaching your students to write, when you introduce new reading skills, and when you teach them phonics. It is the time when you share books, read poems, and incorporate your current theme into reading and writing activities. Literacy learning continues later in the day as part of the Reading and Writing Centers.

> The next step with the reading groups, when the top group will move into reading their first book, is covered in Phase 2-2.

Phase 1-5: Speaking, Reading, and Writing Sentences

Now, a new step begins on the road to reading and writing. During the first two to three weeks of school, with many of the students able to recognize the letters and a good number of sight words, it is time for them to begin reading sentences. All along we have put each new sight word into oral sentences. The stage is set for the class to practice new ways of putting these sight words into oral sentences and then for them to learn to read and write "Sight Word Sentences".

ORAL LANGUAGE DEVELOPMENT

Kindergarten students need many opportunities for oral language development throughout the day. This is best done in whole group situations where teachers have the opportunity to engage students in discussions and news sharing. That way we can model correct language for the students, invite them to join in, listen to them, and guide them. This section contains a variety of oral language activities to use with your class.

Whole class learning has several advantages:

- Students increase their self-confidence when they speak in front of the class.

- They learn language from listening to the teacher and to each other.

- They strengthen their oral language skills.

ORAL COMPOSING OF SENTENCES

Use one or more of the following sentence activities *daily* until the students become familiar with composing sentences in different patterns.

1. Sentence Around a Word

Choose a word, for example the word "like", and say a sentence with the word in it. *"Do you like ice-cream?"*

"Now, you make a sentence with the word 'like'," I tell my students. *"You have to listen to make sure the sentence has 'like' in it."* The first few students tend to compose sentences in the same pattern as the sentence they hear (in this case a question) so give another example using a different pattern: *"I like to play outside."*

Later, when you model writing sentences, the class will be able to *see* the different sentence patterns as well as hear them. This oral composing of sentences can be a five-minute activity, so do it frequently. Before long, the students learn to compose sentences in different patterns.

> *"Can you start your sentence in a different way?"* I ask to encourage the students to vary their sentences. This skill carries over into writing sentences.

2. Sentences About Objects

You need a box with different objects in it: perhaps a pencil, a ruler, a book, a ball, and a ring. Hand them out and say, *"Make a sentence about the object you are holding."*

Accept whatever they tell you with a positive remark, *"Good try!"* If it is not a full sentence, help to finish it or have another student do so.

Record the students saying their sentences on a tape-recorder so that they can hear their own voices. This encourages them to want to participate.

Some children have not yet learned to articulate all the sounds correctly. Before any student can comment or laugh at a mispronunciation, I say, *"Not everyone is able to speak clearly yet. Let's try to help because we want everyone to be happy."* This is usually all it takes to get students to respond positively to the attempts of others.

During oral sentence activities, I know that many ESOL students will not be ready to compose sentences. They need time to develop their ability to speak in English, so I make sure that the whole class repeats the sentences after me. I know that, before long, when they are ready, these students will be making up sentences on their own. The less attention drawn to them, the sooner they will feel free to participate.

3. Finishing Sentence Starts

This is an activity all students love. You can be as inventive as you like with the sentence starts you give them to finish, but try to keep most of the starts within their experience. *"I'm going to begin a sentence, and I would like you to finish it. For example: if I say, 'When I get home, I will…' you might say, ' When I get home, I will have a snack.' Now, think of a different way to finish 'When I get home, I will…'"*

After several students give their sentences, try some other starts: *"We went to the store and…"*

"My mom said, 'You may go outside, but…'"

Try to vary the types of sentence starts you give them. Sometimes just give them a question word such as "Why… ?"

4. Answering Questions in a Sentence

"What is your full name?"

"How old are you?

"Where do you live?"

"What is your phone number?"

"When is your birthday?"

"What is your favorite television program?

"What did you do at the weekend?"

"Who do you play with after school?"

"Why were you absent?"

Encourage your students to rephrase any one-word answers and give you a complete sentence answer, an important skill in grades to come.

READING SIGHT WORD SENTENCES

Introduction

After students understand how to put words together to make oral sentences, they are ready to see sentences being written and then to read them. Written sentences are, after all, the form in which books tell stories and give information. The best way to begin this activity so that your students can be successful, is to start with sentences that are composed of words they already know, along with one or two words that are new. I call these "Sight Word Sentences". (By this time, your top reading group students will already have begun reading "Sight Word Sentences".

They will be able to help others with the sentence reading activities introduced in this chapter.)

Being able to read and write sentences is a very important step for children moving into literacy. These are the same skills they will use when reading books and writing stories.

Goals for this activity:

- to move the children into reading sentences
- to reinforce the concept of "sentence"
- to introduce some new sight words.

1.   Use a few of your sight words to write two sentences on the main classroom chalkboard.

> Example: The boys and girls go to school.
> They are happy.

2.   After writing sentences on the board, always give students a chance to look at the sentences for a minute or so before saying anything. Watch as their faces brighten when they realize they see words they know. After the short pause, they will want to tell you they know some of the words. Give them the chance to come up, point to the words they know, and maybe even read the whole sentence by themselves. You will see their excitement grow as they discover connections by themselves.

3. Then it is time to introduce the new word, "they". This is how I do it:

Introducing New Words

"This is a new word; it says 'they'." Circle the word as you speak.

Read the sentences together, pointing to each word. Then write the word "they" showing the students that it can be written with a capital "T" or a lowercase "t". Tell them it is the same word.

Spend time with the new word, using activities that make the students look at the word closely. For example, have them find little words inside "they"… ("he" and "the") Once you write "he", you can introduce "she". Put them in sentences.

Now, tell them two other "they" sentences. (They go to the door. Where are they?) Have the students give you some of their own "they" sentences.

Next, ask for volunteers to read the sentences while you point. After several students have read, tell them they can read the sentences whenever they want during the week. Post the sentence strips on the board near the Reading Center and keep them there all week.

With the class, read the sentences in the morning and during any five-minute "time-bits". Students are always asking for a chance to go and read a sentence. For many of them, this is their first time to read words in text, and you want them to practice the left to right sweep, pointing to and saying each word,

---

4. For several weeks, write two or three sight word sentences on the board each Monday for the students to read during the week. They should point to the words and read them on their own. Just as you did with the first set of sentences, keep these sentences up for the full week to give all students, especially the ones having difficulty, the chance to have success with this important step.

Taking the Sentences Home

"Keep practicing reading the sentences, because soon you will get to take these sentences home," I tell the students. Their enthusiasm builds.

Here are the next steps:

1. Print the sentences from the board on a sheet of paper and make a copy for each student.

2. On Friday hand these copies out and say, *"Look at your sheet quietly."* Then wait for a few minutes. Soon you will hear voices reading and see faces looking from the sheet to the board. They have made the connection.

3. Ask them, *"What is on your sheet?"* and some of them will tell you that it is the sentences on the board.

   "Now we are going to touch the words and read together." This is a good time to walk around the room watching the students as they read together. Pay close attention to those who will need help. Then give different groups a chance to read.

4. Before you finish, name a few words for the students to find and spell.

5. That afternoon, the time they have been waiting for arrives, and they get to take their first reading sheet home to read to their parents. Soon parents will be telling you how impressed

they are that their child can read the sentences after only three or four weeks in school.

SIGHT WORD SENTENCE EXPLOSION

Fig. 1-5-1:

A student practices reading sentence strips on a pocket chart near the Reading Center.

Now sentences spring up everywhere:

- I write them on my portable chalkboard, which I keep close to where we meet as a whole group on the floor.

- I write them on sentence strips that I place in the sentence strip pocket chart beside the Reading Center.

- I write sight word sentences on strips, cut them into words, and stick magnetic tape on the back for the students to put together again. (Use this as a whole class activity where students go up to the board and unscramble the sentences.)

- I put 2 - 4 sight words on the board. *"Here are some words. Make a sentence with all these words in it."* I say. I write the sentence they give me on the board. When we finish reading over the sentence, we check to make sure all the words are used.

- Students make up sentences by placing flashcards on the floor. Then they read them to their partners.

WRITING SIGHT WORD SENTENCES

It is important to show your students how to write words in a sentence. This also gives you the opportunity to reinforce the proper formation of letters. Earlier, I demonstrated how to write each letter and encouraged students to come to the board and write letters and words and also to practice writing in the Writing Center by copying words from the chart or flashcards.

Now they need to know how to write sentences. It is time for me to model.

> Model all new skills to your students, and I mean *ALL* new skills. Your students will only meet your expectations if you *show* them how. One of the major keys to success with this program is the teacher's role as a model.

I take a sheet of manila drawing paper and turn it so that it is horizontal. Then I crease it horizontally to give more space for these young children to write a sentence. I hand a sheet to each student and make up a sight word sentence that the children can easily relate to and one that they can easily illustrate. The sentence is "I see a fish".

I show the students the crease and tell them, *"Just like you are sitting on your chair, we are going to get these letters to sit on the crease. I know you are going to do a good job. Just watch me and do exactly what I do.*

"Pick up your blue crayon and hold it up. The first word we are going to write is the uppercase 'I'. Watch me. I am going to start at the top and write the "I" and stop just at the crease. Now, it is your turn. Just wave your crayon at me when you are done, and that will tell me you are ready to move on."

"Next, we need a space before we write the word 'see'. Watch to see where I put the 's'." I write the letter 's' and take my "pointer" finger and hold it in the space. Then, I say

to them, *"You write the 's'."* I write the "ee" for them to finish the word.

    "Now we have two words," I say. *"Let's read them together…
'I see'"* I continue modeling the rest of the sentence in the same way and remind them to put in the space before they write the next word.

    When they have finished writing, we go back and read the whole sentence. I show them that, at the end of the sentence, we need to put a little dot that we call a period. I model how to do this, and they put a dot at the end of their sentences, too. Then we go back and look at the sentence. *"The important things to remember about this sentence are that we wrote with the letters sitting on the crease, and we put a space between each word."*

    Then I say, "Draw your finger along the crease to see if all your letters are sitting on it." I draw my finger along, too. At this point I walk around and praise the students for doing such a great job. We talk about what we could draw with this sentence.

    We continue to do this activity during the next few weeks, and the more we do it, the better the students become at writing the letters and writing their own sight word sentences.

- Have students copy sentence strips in the Handwriting Center and take them home.

- Encourage students to write their own sight word sentences in the second Writing Center and then to draw a picture. Later they can share their stories.

Fig. 1-5-2:

A "Sight Word Sentence" story composed in the Writing Center.

> Kindergarten students will only read and write early if we expect them to do so. Start them reading sentences and composing them within the first month of school. It is your expectations that will determine how early your students begin to read.

CONCLUSION

Stop and check. Ask yourself, "How much time did I spend on the activities in this chapter?" because that will determine how much opportunity you have given your children to take off with reading and to take the next step in writing.

Phase 1-6:
Words in Context Everywhere

Fig. 1-6-1: Student circles the words he knows in a "Rhyme on a Sheet".

Finding the words they know in context is a *very important* step for children learning to read. As soon as they know some sight words, they must learn to spot them *everywhere*. The more print-rich your classroom becomes, the more opportunities your students will have to look at text and find words they recognize there. You can imagine the success and excitement they will feel as they find words and read them. This is when they begin to think of themselves as readers.

HELPING STUDENTS TO FIND WORDS IN CONTEXT

1. Using poetry
   Nursery rhymes
   Finger-plays
   Other poems

2. Using books
   Big Books
   Storytime books
   Books in Reading Center

3. Using their environment
4. Using worksheet directions
5. Using children's weekly newspapers

1. USING POETRY

Children love poetry. They love the rhymes, rhythms, and repetitions just as we did when we were little. Use your students' love of the sounds and rhythms of language to help them emerge into literacy. Poems are an important part of this literacy program, so include them in your reading program from the beginning of the year.

Nursery Rhymes

On the second day of the school year, begin to use nursery rhymes and continue to use them for a few weeks. Write the first four to eight lines of a well-known nursery rhyme in large print on a chart.

Goals in using written nursery rhymes:

- to have students discover in the text of each rhyme the sight words they have learned.
- to discuss the print concepts of Title and Characters.
- to have students find the title words inside the rhyme.
- to introduce new sight words.
- to have students enjoy dramatizing the rhymes.

Introducing Nursery Rhymes

1. After saying the rhyme, for example, "Mary Had a Little Lamb", I ask the children, *"Who knows that rhyme?"* Many hands go up. *"Join in if you know it"* I tell them, and we say the rhyme together.

   Then we talk about who is in the story. They hear me refer to Mary and the lamb as characters. We talk about what happened in the rhyme: what happened first, next, etc. I choose two students to act the parts of the characters and hang the character names round their necks before they begin. After the first dramatization of the rhyme, another two students wear the labels and act out the rhyme. (Later in the day, more students can have a turn.)

2. After that, I display the chart and tell them, *"These are the words of the rhyme, and this is the title."*

3. I point to the words and read the rhyme. *"Can you find the names of the characters?"* I ask and call on someone to point to the names. We circle the words "lamb" and "Mary". (In some rhymes they will find the character names several times, so after circling, we count the number of times each character's name appears.)

4. *"What kind of lamb is it?"* I ask. They tell me it is a *little* lamb, so I circle the word "little". At this point, I introduce the word "big".

   "Let's say the poem and instead of using the word 'little', we'll use the word 'big'."

   I write the word "big" on a Post-It and stick it over the word "little". Then we read the rhyme again together, and I ask individual students to come up and point and read.

Students as Peer-Teachers

After the introduction to each poem is over, I move aside and allow students to take over as teachers for the reading of the poems. From the beginning I tell them, _"I am looking for students who are focusing and who can point to the words in the poems slowly so that everybody can read along."_ I model this process for them and have them practice with me until they are able to take over.

During the course of the school year, I can prepare for something else while these students take over the class poetry reading. They are responsible for making sure that their classmates are focusing and reading. Watching them succeed as leaders, reinforces my belief that all it takes is training your students and having high expectations.

Follow-Up: A "Finding Words in Context" Activity

(Also an excellent listening activity)

"Rhymes on a Sheet"

Now it is time for students to see the rhyme in regular-sized print. They each get a sheet of paper with an illustrated version of the nursery rhyme on it. I also have a transparency of this sheet for my overhead projector.

"This is the same nursery rhyme that is on the chart," I tell them pointing to the projected image, _"and it is the same rhyme that you have on your sheet of paper."_

We discuss the picture, and I point to the word "Mary" on the transparency for us to spell together. I circle the word on my transparency and ask them to find it on their sheet and circle it. As I walk around to give assistance, I encourage students to help their neighbors find the word if someone is having difficulty.

We do the same thing with the word "little".

"Now, we are going to color some of the picture together," I tell them. *"Look around the class at the different colored clothes people are wearing. What color do you think Mary's dress could be?"* They decide on blue. I move around as they color the dress. Then we look at shoes and color Mary's shoes black, and finally we color the grass green. Later they will get the chance to finish the picture using whatever colors they want.

> Approaching coloring in this way seems to help the children who have little or no experience with coloring and prevent them from taking one crayon and making random marks all over the paper.

This step-by-step process reinforces the skills of listening and following directions. In a matter of a few weeks, the students produce work that shows more care and improved fine motor control. They are now thinking about their pictures and which colors are appropriate without needing to be "walked through" the task. This simple step-by-step process paves the way for more complex skills later.

With the next few nursery rhymes that we use for this activity, I specify a few parts of the picture for them to color and which colors to use. This gives me the opportunity to teach the colors to students who don't yet know them and to strengthen fine motor skills. By doing this at the very beginning of the year, the children master these skills faster.

Using Finger-Plays

Instead of just saying the finger play rhymes with the actions, you will add more meaning to these action poems if you write the words on a chart for the children. Students love to find the sight words they know in the finger-play poems, and they love to do the actions while the teacher points to the words. This is one more way of incorporating a sight word skill into a fun movement activity. You can even make up your own movement poems. Here is one of mine.

Marching to the Beat

Snap your fingers
Stand up tall
Clap your hands now
One and all.

One, two, three, four
Move your feet.
Now you're marching
To the beat.

I write the finger-plays and movement rhymes on chart paper and post them on the walls. It doesn't take long before the students have a print-rich classroom. They can't help but read, because words they know are all around them in context.

Using Other Poems

Poetry adds such joy to learning that I use many poems in themes throughout the year. Often I introduce two or three poems a week for enjoyment and to fit in with seasonal and learning themes.

As well as reading poems to the class and enjoying them in various ways, I write them on charts and on sheets of paper for students to look at and eventually read. We read and discuss each poem line by line. By reading so much poetry, students are constantly reinforcing old sight words and learning new ones.

Poems form an important part of my class literacy program. They provide supplementary reading material all year and also information to discuss in Circle Time.

So... cut down on "busy-work" time and plug in
      Poetry Time

... read poems to your class in those spare

      five minute "Time Bits".

... copy poems on charts for whole class and

      group "Read the Room" activities.

Choosing Poems

Do not limit the poems you use to those at kindergarten reading level, but choose poems for the children's enjoyment, believing that they will be able to read them. As long as you make the words come alive for students, no word is ever too difficult. Remember that you learned many of the words you read when you were young through seeing them over and over again.

---

2. USING BIG BOOKS AND OTHER STORYTIME BOOKS

During the first week of school when we sit to share our first Big Book, I say to the students, *"Now we are becoming readers. I <u>know</u> you will find words in this book that you can read."*

After we do the "Picture Walk", I read the story through once and say, *"When you were in pre-school, all you did was listen to the teacher read and look at the pictures, but now you can join in with some words and read with me."* Slowly I point to the words and have the students join in with the words they know. Even at this early stage, they find two or three words they know. They also come up to cover part of a word and point out a little word.

Every year, when I open a Big Book for my students, they begin to see words they know. Use as many Big Books as you can during the first few weeks, because you want your students to feel that they are beginning to read. Always give them the opportunity to point out words they know. Every time you do this, you help a child to gain confidence in reading.

Other Books at Storytime

I also read regular-sized books at Storytime. Students first look to see if they know any words in the title. Then they listen for words in the story that they know how to read.

"Listen for the words that you know how to read, and at the end of the story you will get a chance to tell me what words you hear."

QUESTION WORDS AT STORYTIME

Right from the start of the year, whenever I read a story, I often ask the class a few comprehension questions. After a few weeks, I take this one step further. I write the words "What?", "When?", "How?", "Why?", "Where?" and "Who?" on brightly colored 5" x 8" cards. Then I laminate them and post them near the chalkboard where we gather for Storytime. When I ask a question after reading a story, I hold up the flash card of the appropriate question word.

"These are question words," I tell the students. "They help us to think about the stories we read together, so sometimes, when I read a story or poem to you, I will hold up one of these words and ask you a question. I know this smart class will be listening so well that you will be able to answer the questions I ask."

I hold up each question word and name it. They become familiar with them because I use them every day. Later in the year, I let them lift a word and ask a question after a story or poem.

3. USING THE ENVIRONMENT TO FIND WORDS

"These words you are learning to read are everywhere you go," I tell the students, "Look for them. They are around the school. They are on the streets as you drive along. They are in the supermarkets and in the mall, and they are in your home. When you see them, point them out to someone."

And they do. They find words they know on milk cartons at lunchtime and on the cans and cereal boxes in the supermarkets. They find them on road signs and posters, and they tell their parents and share with me. I remind them often to look for words everywhere so that they know it is important.

> When something is important
>
> to you, it becomes important
>
> to your students, too.

Playing "Word Detective" at Home

As early as the first week of school, I ask my students to look at home in magazines and newspapers for the words we have been learning. When they find words they know, they circle the words, cut out a small section around them, and bring them into school. *"Do not cut out words from anything unless you get permission from your parents,"* I remind them. *"Ask your mom and dad for old magazines or newspapers."* Before long they are bringing in sandwich bags full of words they have circled on paper.

4. USING WORKSHEET DIRECTIONS

The students also find sight words on worksheets when I ask them to look for words they know and to circle them. Circling the words they recognize on worksheets leads them into reading the directions. Very soon, no paper comes into their hands without their trying to find and circle words they know.

5. USING STUDENT WEEKLY NEWSPAPERS

Along with books, poems, class-written stories, and Morning News as reading material for the class, I also use one of the weekly children's newspapers (such as the *Weekly Reader*) that can be ordered from publishers. These newspapers provide a source of non-fiction reading material and spark interest in the content amongst these five-year-olds. I also use them as a way to have students recognize and reinforce sight words and punctuation in context.

I introduce the weekly newspaper very early in the year. The children notice that this reading material tells a story. It has pages like a book, and everyone is anxious to find out what the articles have to say each week.

Reading the weekly newspaper is a very special time in my classroom. The children take their places on the rug, and two of them distribute the sheets.

"Sit quietly and look at the paper. You never know... there might be some words here that you recognize."

They start to make connections. Hands shoot up excitedly. " Mrs. McLaughlin, I see the word 'the'." They spot the words "in", "is", "you", etc. I enjoy seeing the excitement in their eyes as they glance back and forth from a word they know in the print on the walls to a word in the paper. (This is just one of the many reasons for having a "print-rich" classroom.)

Everyone wants to identify a word. At the start of the year, a student may be able to match a word in the text with one of the flash card words but not be able to name the word.

When this happens, I show my excitement. *"It is _amazing_ that you remember you have seen this before. It's okay if you don't remember what it says. Can you point to where you see it in the classroom?"* The student goes to point to the word. *"Who can help this smart boy name that word?"* Many hands go up, and I hear little voices saying, "I can." "I know." The word is named.

We progress from page to page and talk about what is happening in the pictures. Even during the first two weeks of school, students are able to recognize at least one word on every page. At the beginning, I assist students to identify words by writing on the chalkboard the words they discover in the text. Seeing the words in larger print helps them to make the connection. They can now match these words with words in the newspaper.

Their final activity is to go back to their seats and circle or highlight the words they know. At this time I move around the classroom. I want to spend quality time with students who have shown they are on the way but are not making the connections yet. I talk to them about what they have learned and try to build their enthusiasm and confidence.

Sometimes I bring over two or three flashcards and ask them to match those words with words in their newspaper. By doing this, I help them to feel they are a part of the group instead of being discouraged that they are not able to find words on their own.

Each week students are able to circle more and more words. This progress not only reinforces the words but also leads them to believe that they will soon be able to read the whole newspaper by themselves. That is my goal.

CONCLUSION

At the beginning of kindergarten, print doesn't mean much to these young children. You can hang your poems, charts, Morning News, and stories around the room, but that will not in itself bring joy and success in learning to read unless the print comes alive to the students. When children find sight words they know in the rhymes, charts, news, etc., they become excited. It is up to you, the teacher, to catch that excitement and keep it moving… and not to lose any student and not to leave anyone behind.

This finding of words they recognize in context is a very important step in children learning to read. It is the time when they first realize that they *really* are reading. You have to keep them believing they are readers, you have to keep them moving, and you have to share in their excitement. Reinforce with individual and specific praise, because every child must feel important and successful.

How quickly we could overlook the tiny steps of those children who might only know a few sight words. Remember that some of the children taking tiny steps at the start of the year will be your highest achievers. All they need is time to grow and for you to keep showing them that you believe in them.

Phase 1-7:
Introducing Letter Sounds

When learning to recognize the letters is underway, I begin to teach letter-sounds. It is much easier for children to learn the sounds if we look at two letters at a time. Having two sounds to compare helps students to differentiate between them. I begin this process with a picture/letter-sound matching activity.

PICTURE TO LETTER-SOUND MATCHING

1. Choose two letter sounds. (It is a good idea to choose two letters to introduce together whose sounds are very different. For example: "s" and "b".) Gather about six pictures to go with each letter-sound of the alphabet you work with. Divide the chalkboard in two with a vertical line.

2. Write the "s" on one side and the "b" on the other. Point to the letter "s" and say the sound. Then have the students say it with you. Do the same thing with the "b".

3. Tell the students that you have some pictures that start with the "s" sound or the "b" sound. Hand them out.

4. Have each child in turn hold up a picture. The class names it together.

5. Now model what you want them to do. It is important to model in complete sentences.

> *"This is a picture of the sun.*
> *Sun begins with sss (s sound).*
> *I'll put the picture under the letter 's'."*

6. Give each student with a picture the chance to name the picture, say the sound, and place it under the appropriate letter.

7. When all the pictures are placed on the board, take them off and distribute them to others who have not had a chance to try.

8. Write the name of the object beside each picture on the board. Ask, *"Do you notice anything about all the words under the letter 's'?"* Someone will notice that they all begin with "s". Ask the same question about the words under the letter "b". Keep the pictures on the board all week for students to practice with.

Follow-Up Writing Activity

• Tell the students that they are going to write some of the words on the board and draw the pictures that go with them.

• Fold some sheets of paper in four, and hand them out.

• Tell your students, *"Lift your crayons. Watch me as I write each letter. You are going to write it after me."* Write the two "s" words chosen, letter by letter, one on each top quarter of the paper, and the two "b" words on the bottom quarters.

• Now tell the children that they will draw a picture to go with the word in each box, and model this drawing for them. Don't forget to praise students' work as they write and draw.

MORE FUN WITH LETTER-SOUNDS

Three "Gathering" Activities

1. Call each table of students in turn to sit on the rug in front of the chalkboard and make the sound of the letter "p": p-p-p. The students join in making the sound as they come to sit and keep making the sound until everyone is seated. Now call on a student to write the letter for the sound.

2. Write a letter on the board or hold up a letter card and have the students make the sound as the class gathers.

3. Post three letters on the board as the class gathers and select a student. That student can pick up any letter, name the letter, say the sound, and give a word that begins with the sound.

Note:

All the letter card games in "Phase 1-2: Learning the Letters & Training Students as Peer-Teachers" can be adapted to practice letter-sounds. As well as naming the letter, have the students make the sound and say a word that begins with the sound.

CHECKING ON THE LEARNING

After you have introduced several sounds and the students have had time to consolidate this learning, you can use another copy of the alphabet sheets that you used to record letter recognition and mark which letter-sounds each student knows. Once all sounds have been taught, it is time to check to find out which sounds each student still has to master. After you assess each student, you can plan further class teaching or individual time with the students who need help.

> Because vowel sounds are more difficult for students to learn, I start with consonants and teach the short vowel sounds later.

CONCLUSION

Normally, at two letter-sounds a week, it would take about three months to get through the alphabet. Because I use other activities and the students increasingly listen to sounds in the words they want to write, most students know the letter-sounds long before three months is over.

Phase 1-8:
Reading and Writing Centers

Included in the centers that I set up in the classroom during the first two weeks (housekeeping, blocks, puzzles, art, clay, etc.) are the Reading and Writing Centers. These Reading and Writing Centers are an important and active part of my literacy program.

They provide places where students can...

- practice the literacy skills they are learning.
- work cooperatively in groups.
- stretch their skills and explore.
- expand their oral language.

In the Reading and Writing Centers, students can work independently or together, sharing their thoughts and ideas. By observing your students and working with them in your centers, you can discover much about each child and how he or she learns.

STARTING CENTER TIME

I put the students into groups of three, mixing abilities and talents, knowing that they will learn from each other. Soon they know to stay with their group until I flick the lights for them to stop and clean up their center.

These are not permanent groups. However, it is helpful to keep the same groups for a while at the start of the year. After that, the students will have free choice of center on certain days. There are several benefits for keeping the children in the same groups for a while: they get to know each other, they bond with each other, and they become partners in learning. Soon they feel free to speak their thoughts with the others in their group.

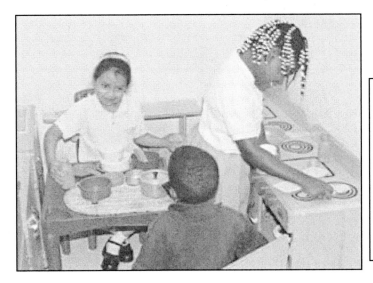

Fig. 1-8-1:

All centers give opportunities for building students' oral language with new social and learning vocabu-lary.

At the start of the year, I allow twenty minutes each day for Center Time. I post the centers on the board and, under each center's name, place a list of a few students, usually three depending on how many students there are in each class. The groups are rotated to the next center each day. Color-coding the name cards helps students identify their groups at the start of the year.

SETTING UP AND USING THE WRITING CENTER

My Writing Center has two separate areas:

1: Handwriting

At this center are pieces of chalk, small portable chalk-boards, and chalk erasers. I also place a set of letter flashcards and a list of the sight words they are learning to read. Before the groups go to their centers, I model what they can do. I tell them that this is where they can write letters and write words.

"Watch me write some words," I say.

Slowly I write a few words on my chalkboard. Then I give two or three children a chance to sit at the center and write so that the others can see how they do it. After all have finished, they hold up their chalkboards for the class to see, and I congratulate them on doing a good job.

At this first area, I also have handwriting sheets to help students practice individual letters if they are having difficulty with them.

2: Composing with Writing

The second part of the Writing Center is where students can make up their own stories… their favorite part of writing. At this center are crayons, pencils, and sheets of paper.

At the start of the year, I tell the students that this is where they get to draw their own stories, and if they want to write words in the story, they can. Then I show them how to do this.

First, I tell them a short story. For example: *"I went to the playground with my friend. We played on the swings, and we slid down the slide."* I ask them to name some things they might find on the playground. Then I draw a picture for them of two children on a playground with some of the things they mention.

When I finish, I post my picture so that they have an example of what to do. Later, when the students share their work with the class, I show them how some children wrote letters or words as well as drawing pictures. The next day, I model writing words along with a drawing.

I encourage the students to make up any story they want when they are at this center. *"Even if you don't have a story about yourself, just make up any story and draw it,"* I tell them.

Early student Writing Center stories often contain drawings with strings of letters and words. These students already know

81

that stories are made up of letters and words, so they use some of the letters and words they see around them.

Fig. 1-8-2 (Side) In the Writing Center near the start of the year, a student has added letters and words copied from around the room to his picture story.

Fig. 1-8-3: (Below) A student has drawn a picture story and then added several repeated strings of words.

Starting Student Writing Portfolios

This is the time to begin collecting samples of your students' writing as a tool for assessing progress. Start a folder for each student and put this first writing sample in the folder to begin the year. Then you will need to add dated samples of each stage of their writing.

These portfolios are valuable tools. They help me to see how far the students have come, and they are useful at parent conferences.

SETTING UP AND USING THE READING CENTER

My Reading Center is always located near the chalkboard and next to a reading wall where many of the charts are posted. Children love to pretend to be teachers, so I place pointers for them to use when they read from the charts around the print-rich room. The sight word pocket chart is nearby. During this first phase of the Reading Center, I place sets of flashcards with letters and sight words there for the students to practice with. They can practice reading any of the materials we have worked on. Later, when they begin to read books, I set up a reading table with books for independent reading.

THE TEACHER'S ROLE DURING CENTER TIME

Although there is so much else to accomplish during my day, and I could use this time to do other things, Center Time is very important to my teaching. It gives me the opportunity to learn more about the students as I visit with them at the centers, especially the Reading and Writing Centers.

At the beginning of the year, Center Time gives me a little over five minutes with each child in a group to help them reinforce the sight words. Often, during class literacy time, students would love to have me listen to them identify sight words or to give me a sentence using a flashcard word, but there is not enough time to hear them all before the literacy period is over. I tell the children I will listen to them later. Center Time gives me the chance to do so.

Later on, when they begin to read books, I use Reading Center time to give individual students a jump start on the next day's reading by introducing them to a new book and listening to them read.

In the Writing Center, I observe and encourage students as they write, giving assistance as needed. I also listen while they tell me about their picture stories.

USING THEMES IN READING AND WRITING CENTERS

I use the thematic approach to enhance literacy skills and other learning throughout the year and bring the themes into some of the Center Time activities. This gives me the opportunity to include reading and writing in creative ways with art, crafts, music, and movement. Here are some of the themes I use: Dental Health, Nutrition, Thanksgiving, Famous Americans, Farm Animals, Zoo Animals, Ocean Animals, Insects, and Multicultural Awareness themes.

Along with having the students read books on these themes and write about some of the interesting topics we discuss, I use as many poems and songs as I can find on each topic and post the words of these poems and songs on charts around the room. Also, I make information charts, which, later in the year, include pictures and a paragraph of five or six sentences for each topic. Students often read the wall charts during Center Time. They draw and write about the theme topics as well.

CONCLUSION

Soon all the centers have been established, and the students trained in how to use them. Center Time quickly becomes one of the most popular times of the day, when the students enjoy exploring to find what they can do, and when they have the freedom to try out their own ideas. In the small, mixed ability groups, they learn from each other and help each other. Although I encourage students to work independently during Center Time and know that this is their time to explore, I am always aware of what is going on. I make sure that learning is taking place, and that they are talking, working, and playing happily together.

End of Phase One

Phase Two

"Building on the Foundation"

In Phase Two the students will move into reading books. They will build their phonics skills, and they will learn to compose short stories and write their journals.

Phase 2-1:
Reading and Composing Short Stories

Now that the students are used to composing and reading sight word sentences, it is time to expand reading and writing with "Story of the Week". In the activities that follow, students learn to read and write simple three or four-sentence stories.

SHARED READING OF A "STORY OF THE WEEK"

The Goals of this Shared Reading activity are:

- to extend reading single sentences into reading a simple, short story written by the teacher to fit in with the theme being used in class that week.
- to expand the students' vocabulary.
- to show that each sentence begins with a capital.
- to review the use of a period at the end of a sentence.
- to take students step-by-step through illustrating the story.

Introducing "Story of the Week"

The first step is to prepare a three-sentence story using some of the sight words the students have been learning. Though this will probably link in with whatever theme you are using with your class during the week, it can be a story about anything you choose. I write the story on a half-chart page. (You can see samples of "Stories of the Week" in Appendix C)

On the first day of the week, I show them the story I wrote. *"I have a story for you. It is about fall. Look at the story, and see how many words you can recognize."*

Within a minute, hands are shooting up, and I call them to come to the chart and point to the words they have found.

Next, we read the story together.

Fall is here.
Look at the leaves.
They are red, orange,
   yellow, and brown.

Because the "Story of the Week" will usually go with your theme, you can incorporate reading it with other lessons during the week. I post it in front of the class, so that every time we gather on the rug, we can read it together. As you read the story with the class repeatedly during the week, it is almost impossible for the students not to recognize new words and know their meaning. If you take the new words and use them in other contexts, you are helping to broaden the students' understanding. For instance, with the word "here" I might say the following sentences to show how it could be used:

<u>Here</u> is my book.
<u>Here</u> is his chair.
They are <u>here</u>.
Is Johnnie <u>here</u> today?

GUIDED ILLUSTRATION OF THE "STORY OF THE WEEK"

- Later that same week, I write the story on the bottom of a letter-sized sheet of paper leaving the top half for illustration. Then I make a copy for each child.

- On Friday, with the students sitting on the floor, I pass out the story sheet to them. We read the story together.

- *"Now you are going to draw a picture about your story. What should we put in the picture?"*
    "Leaves," some tell me.
    "Trees," others say.
    "Watch me," I say and draw some bare trees with a brown crayon. *"What colors will the leaves be?"* I ask. They tell me the four colors of the leaves, and I draw some leaves on the trees and some on the ground, Then I color them red, orange, yellow, and brown.

- *"Now, it is your turn to illustrate your story"* I tell them. *"I know you're going to do a good job with your picture. Remember, you can draw your own picture whatever way you want. Your trees and leaves do not have to look like mine."*

    They start their pictures. I move around as they work, helping and encouraging. *"I don't know how to draw,"* a little voice tells me, and I spend some time with that student as he tries to draw.

- When they have finished, the students at each table stand and show their pictures. Sure enough, most of the drawings are different. *"I'm so glad you used your own brains,"* I tell them. *"You're doing a great job. I knew everybody could do it."* I give special recognition to the students who were having difficulty.

- Then it is time to hang all the illustrated stories on a wall of the classroom. The students are very proud to see their work displayed. The stories stay up for a week, after which, I put a copy in their work sample portfolios and send the story home for them to read to their parents.

    You will find that by reading a new story every week, your students' reading vocabulary will expand, and soon your room will be filled with meaningful material that your students can read… and not with commercially made posters that they do not understand.

The firefighter is our friend.

He comes in a big red fire truck.

He puts the fire out.

Fig. 2-1-1: This "Story of the Week", written to go with a class "Community Helpers" theme, has been illustrated by a student who will take it home to read to his parents. These weekly, three or four sentence stories help to prepare students for reading books.

There are many kinds of ladybugs. Some are red with spots. Some are orange with spots and some don't have spots at all. They are all welcome in the garden. Do you know why?

Fig. 2-1-2:

"Story of the Week" goes on almost every week for the rest of the year. By April, the walls are filled with stories written on the many different themes the class has studied. The one on the left was written for a "Bugs" theme.

One purpose for keeping these story charts on display is that the students can use them to find the spellings of words they want to write.

TEACHING STUDENTS TO COMPOSE STORIES

I show the class a picture, for example a bear. The picture can link in with your class theme if you wish.

"What will we call this bear?" I ask. They suggest names, and we pick one. I show them how to write the title *Sleepy Bear* in the center at the top of a chart page.

1. Next we discuss where the bear might live and some of the things he might do. I write the sentences they give me on the chalkboard as they say them to me, and together we decide which three sentences we will put into our story that day. I make sure they know that stories can have any number of sentences in them, but for now we are just writing three.

2. *"Watch carefully,"* I tell them. I write my first sentence on the chart and stop to remind them about the word space and

that the first word starts with an uppercase letter, and there is a period at the end of the sentence.

3.   *"Now, watch as I write the other sentences, and remind me to put a period at the end because sometimes I forget."*

> Sleepy Bear is brown.
> He is funny.
> He lives at the zoo.

4.   When I finish writing, making sure I forget the periods so they have to remind me, we read through the story together. *"Now, let's check to make sure that all the sentences make sense and all the sentences are about the bear."* I say. We read the first sentence, and I ask, *"Does that sentence make sense?"* and *"Is it about Sleepy Bear?"*

   "Yes," they tell me.

   We do the same with the other two sentences. This shows students what they should do after they finish any story. It helps them acquire the habit of reading through their work to check it after they finish writing.

5. Last of all, I invite two or three students to come up and point to the words while the others read.

We continue to create stories together as a class. The more we do this, the better the students participate and the better they become at understanding how to put their thoughts down on paper. Within two or three weeks of starting this activity, their thoughts flow more freely, and some of them are able to dictate a whole story of several sentences without help.

CENTER TIME:

STUDENTS WRITE THEIR OWN STORIES

"You are thinking of so many sentences that I'm sure you will soon be able to write stories on your own," I tell the students. In front of the class, I fold several sheets of blank

paper in half. Then I remind them, *"Write the story on the bottom and illustrate the story on the top half, just like we did with these displayed pages."* Then I put the sheets in the Writing Center for them to use later if they wish.

For the next few days, I visit the Writing Center during Center Time until I have met with all the groups. This is important follow-up. It enables me to encourage students to write a story, to be there to help build their confidence as they try this new skill. What they are really doing here is using the sight words to form sentences for a very short story. They will say the sentences in their stories and ask how they write a particular word that they want to use. Some of them are "pretend writing" and others are really trying to put words together to compose their story.

> There is a purpose for every step I take, so I know I must make time to be with my students when they first try out a new skill. I know that if I just leave the folded paper in the Writing Center, some children would not even make an attempt at writing.

THE IMPORTANCE OF STUDENTS SHARING WRITING

When your students write at the Writing Center, make sure that they share their pictures and stories with you in a brief conference at the end of Center Time. In this way you can reinforce the steps they take and guide them to the next step.

Also, when you next sit together as a class, have the students read their stories aloud and tell everyone what their illustrations are about. Give them positive feedback yourself, and encourage other students to say what they like about the reader's story and picture. Then proudly post the stories where everyone can see. (Remember to keep adding samples of your students' writing to their portfolios. This will be your way of assessing their progress.)

Sharing time is to encourage the students to "open up", express themselves, and feel good about themselves. It will also show them what the others are trying. This affirming process can be done in just a few minutes with a few students sharing at a time. Sharing their writing aloud in front of the class empowers students and gives them a "voice".

> The more recognition and positive feedback your student-writers get, the more motivation they will have to write again and write often. Soon, before you know it, they will *all* be writing and illustrating.

CONCLUSION

At this time, you will notice that your students can read many, many sight words and are trying to put these words into their own sentences. Soon, more students will speak up to offer ideas in this class story-writing experience and to help you spell the words that they know. Soon, some of the stories that students write at Center Time will be several sentences long, and a few students may even "take off" into longer stories.

Fig. 2-2-1: Students in a group point and read in unison from a reproducible book.

LET'S TAKE A LOOK AT WHERE THE STUDENTS ARE IN LEARNING

Now that several weeks have passed, it is a good time to pause and look at where the students are. They have been in school since mid-August, and they have learned a lot:

- The alphabet sheets are full of smiley faces. Some students are working hard with certain letters, but most have finished with this skill.

- Everyone can recognize many sight words.

- They are reading sentences, short class-made stories, and the poems and charts on the walls.

- They can identify sight words in their worksheets and weekly newspaper.

- They are getting better at writing letters, words, and sentences.

- Some are listening for sounds in the words they want to write.

- They are helping each other and building teamwork skills.

- Their fine motor skills are making good progress.

- They participate more freely in discussions.

- Their listening and focusing skills are improving.

- Most students have acquired the habit of working quickly and finishing on time with the class.

Already they have come a long way. From all the reading they have been doing, some students are now ready to be launched into book reading. Others are not quite there yet, and a few are still taking tiny steps. As they all make progress with emergent literacy skills, I keep in mind the need to continue building teamwork and the students' ability to take responsibility for each other. Group reading of books will help.

1. CHOOSING THE FIRST GROUP

Through observing the students at Group Reading Time as they make progress reading the sentence strips on the pocket chart, I identify the students who are ready to move into reading books. Most of them have mastered all the new sentence strips I have placed in the pocket chart during the last few days. They have shown me that they can read the sentences in the "Story of the Week" charts on the wall. They can also identify some words in the poem charts. I select which three or four students from the most advanced group will be the first book readers.

2. CHOOSING BOOKS

The first book I select for this group has eight to ten pages with each page having pictures and two to three lines of text in fairly large print. Most of the words are sight words the students already know. Almost any book that meets these requirements will do. I use both trade books and reproducible books from a literacy series. With the reproducible books, I find I need to use the first grade series, as the kindergarten books have only a few words on each page. However, when my "tiny step" students are ready to read books, I will find an easier reproducible book that is not as advanced for them to start reading.

By this time, the class has been exposed to so many sight words, poem charts, and "Stories of the Week" that I do not use the early emergent books that have one-sentence pages with repetitious phrases throughout the book. Those books do not hold the students' interest because most students have advanced further than this in reading. All too often, children are not reading the one line repetitious books so much as memorizing them.

Do not be too quick to think of reproducible books as being poor cousins of the more colorful and appealing trade books. I have several reasons for using them along with trade books. First, they have a controlled vocabulary that accumulates and reinforces itself from the earliest book in the series. They also provide a low-cost solution for schools with limited fund-ing. Last of all, students can have a copy of each of these books to take home and keep.

The joy these young children experience in having a repro-ducible copy to take home as their own book can help them begin a lifetime of loving to read. These may be the only books some young students have been able to call their own. By the end of the school year, many of these children will have up to sixteen of these books in a bag. I have found that children who leave kindergarten with a bag of books to take home, come back after the long summer break reading even better than before. Note, however, that I only use reproducible books for a while to get students into reading, and I always integrate trade books that are more colorful and exciting.

Usually, I buy five or six copies of each trade book to begin with and constantly add to my collection. An important consideration in acquiring books is to make sure you always have books at the next difficulty level ready for the groups to move into. As much as possible, choose fiction and non-fiction books that the children will love because of three factors: the ways they can relate to the story, the fun with language in the way the stories are told, and the attractive illustrations in the book.

3. LAUNCHING THE FIRST GROUP

When I launch the first group into reading books, I use this as an opportunity to give the other groups a look at what goes on and a glimpse into what they will be doing soon. I copy the pages of the first book onto overhead transparencies. Then I bring the whole class up to sit in front of the chalkboard.

I show them the first book and tell them. *"This is the first book you will read in your group. Tomorrow, some of the people reading sentence strips will get to read this book. I know that many of you will recognize some of the words in it."*

We read the title together and discuss what they think the book will be about from looking at the cover picture. Then, one page at a time, we look at the pictures in the book and talk about what is going on.

"Watch me point to the words and read through this whole book," I tell them.

I read each page and then invite them to read along with me as much as they can. Next, I invite the first students who will be reading this book to read the beginning two pages aloud by themselves while the others look on,

"Didn't they do a great job. Let's give them a cheer. Soon you will all be able to read like that. I have one of these books for each of you. Practice hard in your reading groups, because, before you know it, it will be your turn."

During Center Time that same day, I pull the top group to practice reading the book together. This will prepare them for the next day. *"Tomorrow, in Group Reading Time you will get to read the book that the class read with me this morning."* I tell them. *"Here it is. Each of you will have your own copy. First, I want you to read with me when I point to the words."* I point and we all read together. Then, I hand each of them a book.

Now, it is time for them to try reading together as a group without me. *"Just as you read together with me, now you have to read together as a group. Nobody should be reading ahead of the others. You need to say the same words at the same time."* They practice for a few minutes while I watch.

"You're doing a great job," I tell them. *"I can't wait until you read this whole book to the class. You will give them a big surprise."*

Before ending the session, I say to them, *"Let me see how well you can find words on the pages. Go to page one. Who can find the word 'is'?"* Once a student finds it, I wait until the others find it, too, and we spell the word together. It is important to do this with several words on each page.

"You are such a smart group. I am so impressed," I tell the students at the end of the session.

Giving students the chance to find words on each page and spell them aloud together lets you know if they are identifying the new words. It also gives them more practice with reading those words. I use this technique all through the year.

101

4. THE FIRST GROUP MODELS

The next day after Group Reading Time, I gather the whole class on the rug with the three book-readers standing in front of them holding their books. *"Boys and girls, I have a surprise for you,"* I announce. The three new book readers beam with anticipation. They just can't wait to show off what they know.

"These students have learned to read the whole book, and they want to read it to you," I proudly tell the class. I set three chairs in front of the class for the readers. *"Now, watch them point to the words and read together,"*

While the three read, I stand behind them to give them support. They read slowly through the book turning the pages. I encourage them to stop and show the pictures.

"Give them a big hand," I tell the class. *"Can you believe it? They are only in kindergarten a short while, and they already know how to read this hard book. Are they smart or what?"*

"Yes, they are smart," the other students tell me.

"This whole *class is smart, and everyone will get to read this book,"* I say. I hold up other copies of the book. *"I am looking for more top students to learn to read this book. Let me see the hands of people who think they are ready."*

Hands go up everywhere. "I want to try!" "I want to try!" they say.

"Tomorrow, during our reading time, I will pick some more students to read with these super kids."

5. ADDING MORE GROUPS

- The next morning at reading time, the group of book readers can't wait to get together and read their books. I give them a chance to practice for a few minutes. *"You have done a great job,"* I tell them. *"You still remember how to touch the words and read together."* I show them another book. *"This is the book you will read next. But first, you have to teach some students how to read the book you have just read."*

- One way I do this is to bring over three more students, and assign one to each of the students in the first group. *"Sit beside your partner and read with them as they point. Soon it will be your turn to do the pointing,"* I tell them and spend some time reading together with the three pairs of students.

  (If you prefer, instead of assigning the three new students to the previous three and having a top group of six students, these three could be another reading group.)

- *"Now, I am going to check on the other groups. When I come back, I will listen to how you are doing. If your partners are able to point to the words and read, they will get their own books."*

     The reason I leave is to give the students a chance to develop independence in the group. I want them to focus and stay on task. When I am away from them, I constantly check back to encourage and praise them. That is what makes the magic.

- After several minutes I return to the group. *"Are you ready to read for me?"* I ask. By this time they are all ready to show me that they can point and read. I watch them do this.

     "I am so impressed," I tell them. *"I was watching you and saw you talking quietly, and as soon as I reminded you, you went back to reading. No wonder you did such a good job. Now, everyone gets a book. Now, we will have six people reading the book together with everybody holding their own book."* Their faces light up as the three new students get their books.

A LOOK AT ALL THE GROUPS DURING GROUP READING TIME

Group 1

These are the six students who are now reading their first book. This number will vary.

Group 2

This group is preparing to move into reading books. They are reading sentence strips located in the pocket chart. These sentences are made up of high frequency words and words they will encounter in their first books. The goal is to identify these words in context and also practice the left to right sweep. All sentences should be composed to be meaningful to the children.

Group 3

This group is reading vocabulary words that include many of the high frequency words they will encounter in reading. I encourage the students to identify the words and make sentences around them with their partners. They are also reading simple class-made stories.

The Other Groups

The number of these groups varies. Students will team up to learn sight words, and, from time to time, my assistant and I will pull students to work individually or in small groups to reinforce letter recognition.

SOME THOUGHTS ABOUT GROUP STRUCTURE

Having several groups, each working at the level of its students' ability to learn, gives a flexible structure to my reading time that allows me to move individual students on when I see they are ready. It is important that learning does not stagnate.

The students know to which group they belong. They know where to go and what to do each morning without needing to be reminded. As soon as the school "in-house" news is over, they move quickly to their groups. The motivation is there for them to master the skills, to show they respect each other, and to show me they can focus. They know that, as soon as I see they show mastery in what they are doing, they will be moving on, and they constantly ask me when they will do this.

Yes, the steps are there for them to move up into reading books, and soon these steps (that include the reading of sight words, class stories, and sentence strips) will be phased out as all the children move into reading books.

It is important that the students are seeing text and reading *every* day.

> Once students are able to read a book, I don't want them to spend day after day reading the same material that they have already mastered. They need to move on to the next book. The need to move on is the same with the students reading sentence strips and those reading vocabulary words. They all need to feel they are making progress.

WHEN A NEW STUDENT ENTERS THIS STRUCTURE

When new students come into my class at this stage, I check to see where they are in reading. Some may not know the letters of the alphabet yet, but I do not limit them to learning the letters first, I move right into teaching them sight words that they can relate to (always remembering to build oral sentences around these words). This allows the new students to feel successful and to believe they are reading. It helps to pair new students with buddies who can help them.

Motivation is so high with this literacy model that it takes most students a matter of a few weeks to make their way through the steps of learning the letters and being able to read sight words and sentence strips. Many of these students were ready to learn to read but had not been exposed to teaching techniques that would lead them to success. Parents have been amazed at how quickly their children become readers after transferring into classrooms where this model is being used.

WHAT ESOL/ESL STUDENTS DO DURING READING TIME

ESOL/ESL students are usually in my classroom during the class literacy time. Later in the day, they go to special classes that help them to learn English. I have found that I don't need to treat these students differently. With the constant modeling by teacher and students that goes on in my room from the start of school, they catch on to most skills quickly. It is much easier for them to "catch on" when they come into our school system in kindergarten where the children begin to learn to read and write.

Fig. 2-2-2: ESOL/ESL students read together in the same way as the other students in the class.

The only difference I see with ESOL students is that they are just learning to express themselves in English and so do not immediately join in with class discussions. That comes later. But, as far as learning sight words and reading sentences and books are concerned, they learn along with the other students. Perhaps this is because of the joyful, risk-free atmosphere in the classroom and perhaps it is also due to the cooperative learning that takes place. These young students feel free to learn.

Many assume that when ESOL students enter the classroom, they have to focus heavily on oral language and pictures, but with this model these students learn to identify sight words early, just like their English speaking classmates. Comprehension of English and the ability to express themselves in English takes longer. While those skills are underway, the students have learned to read many sight words and are moving into reading books.

CHECKING UP ON THE LEARNING

Remember that checking on the learning should not wait until months have gone by. It should be on-going. Informal assessment goes on continuously as you work with your students every day. Assessment is the only way that you can know where the students are in learning and which skills individual students have mastered. Your school will have assessment tools that you are required to use that will help you to check up on your students' learning.

I begin using Reading Running Records with my students as soon as I see they are ready. These Running Records go on until the end of the school year.

CONCLUSION

Very quickly, within a month after starting the book-reading process, most of the students are reading books. By January each year, even students in the lowest group are doing some form of book reading. Once they have mastered the first book, they move on to the next, and they will continue this pattern of advancing to the next difficulty level for the rest of the year.

The Importance of Consistency

What brought the students successfully to this point are the little steps we took. One followed the other and yet they were part of the whole, and they continue together as a whole. The glue that binds the little steps together and enables the children to flow on into reading books, is *consistency*.

Children do not learn the classroom rules merely by listening to the teacher go over the rules on the first day of school. It is the continuous reinforcement of the rules and the praising of student efforts that make the rules work. The same strategy brings success with training your students and with reading and writing. When you introduce a behavior or skill, you have to reinforce it *consistently*. Just as you watch for the students who are improving their behavior, you watch for the students moving forward in learning, and, whether they take great strides or little steps, you cheer them on for each step they take.

<u>Sustaining the Forward Momentum</u>

You also have to be consistent in moving each student on to his or her next step, keeping in mind that each is an individual who needs to make progress in his or her own way.

You have to know what your goals are for each student, because, if you stop including any child in your focus, that child will stop moving forward. By ignoring any child's needs, you may be setting the student up for frustration and failure.

Phase 2-3:
Writing News & Listening for Sounds

IT'S TIME TO INTRODUCE WRITING NEWS.

Since the beginning of the year, the students have shared their news orally with the class during Circle Time. I have encouraged them to share news about themselves and also to talk about the news they see on television. Once they begin to identify letter sounds and then experience "Story of the Week", I invite them to assist me in writing our class journal (Morning News).

It is important at this stage, early in the year, to show your students how to listen to the initial and ending sounds in the words they want to write and then to write down the letters for these sounds. Every year, there are always a few students who come into kindergarten knowing the letter-sounds. They are ready for this next step in writing, so why wait?

Fig.2-2-1: You can see from this work done in the Writing Center during the first three weeks of school, that this student has already begun to sound out the words she wants to write. She is not just writing sight words or words from around the classroom. She and others like her are ready to be moved on.

What about the students who aren't ready? Don't worry. All students will catch on to this skill in their own time.

Meanwhile, each student will benefit at his or her own level from seeing this process modeled. Some will have letter recognition reinforced, some will have letter-sounds reinforced, and others, who already know the letters and their sounds, will be able to listen for the sounds in each word and write the letters down.

<u>My goals for this activity are</u>...

- to encourage students to participate in oral sharing.

- to give ESOL/ESL students a chance to share and have their friends translate if needed.

- to apply the students' growing letter-sound knowledge.

- to show students how to write and illustrate their own news stories.

- to enable students to reinforce words commonly used in writing their news.

- to provide more reading material that is meaningful for the class.

WRITING NEWS: MODELING FOR THE CLASS

- After the students have shared their news at Circle Time, I say, *"Now, I am going to share my news with you. Are you listening? 'I went home. I ate dinner. Then I watched the news.'"*

    "Now listen again and see if you can hear any words you know." I slowly repeat my story. They tell me they hear the word "I". I touch myself and say, "I". Then I point to the uppercase "I" on the letter charts above the chalkboard. *"Whenever you are talking about yourself, always use the uppercase 'I'."* On the chart I write the uppercase "I".

- *"What word is next?"* I repeat the whole sentence. They tell me "went". We make the beginning sound together, and I call on a student to say the letter. Then I write the "w" on the chart. Next, we listen to the ending sound, and they tell me "t". I write the "t" beside the "w".

112

- We read what we have written so far, *"I wt… What comes next?"* "Home" they say. They listen in turn for the beginning and ending sounds, and I write the letters as they name them "hm" and then put a period, reminding them to put a period at the end of their sentences, too.

- We continue to write the other two sentences with students listening for the sounds and helping me with the letters.

- When the story is finished, we read it together. I point out the space between each word and remind them that whenever we write our stories, we have to leave the word space.

Teachers often ask me, "How do you get your students to space their words so well early in the year?" I tell them that it takes persistence and begins the first day they start modeling writing for their students. That's the time to show students how to put in the word space. Then, every time they come up to write a sentence on the board for the class to see, remind the student again to put a finger space after each word.

> It is important not to correct the spelling of these young students as they emerge into writing. This is the time to allow their thoughts to flow and for you to receive positively what they produce. Their ability to spell words will grow as they learn to read more words and to listen for sounds in the words they write.

STUDENTS WRITE THEIR OWN NEWS

The next day, I write a student's news story with the class, again having them help by naming the letters for the sounds they hear in each word.

- Then I hand out a sheet of blank paper to each child. *"Write your story on the bottom and illustrate on top,"* I tell them, showing them where and encouraging them to draw something about their news.

- As they write, I wander around, encouraging them and saying, *"Tell me what you are writing."*

    Although some children are writing strings of letters, I see many students stopping to say words and listen to the sounds. Some students begin their sentences by saying "I" and their thoughts make sense. When I notice this and listen to their sentences, I know that they have made the connection between having a thought and writing it on paper. I accept whatever the students produce. What is important at this stage is that they can tell me what they have written.

SHARING THEIR WRITING AND ILLUSTRATIONS

When the students have all finished, we gather in a big circle on the floor, and they have the chance to read their stories and tell about the pictures. As I said in "Phase 2-1: Reading and Composing Short Stories", it is important to make sure that all children feel good about their writing.

Every time we share writing, I model how to give positive feedback and remind the class to keep their comments positive, too. While many of the comments will be about the whole story or picture at first, I show them that a comment can be about one particular thing. You will find that when you comment positively on something specific a child has done in his or her writing it helps to encourage other students to try this, too.

For example: *"I like the way you remembered to write an uppercase 'I' when you wrote the word 'I'. That was smart."*

or *"Jasmine, I like the way you listened for the sounds in words to help you spell. You did such a good job that I know what your story says."*

> This individual news-writing activity tells me much about my students. When I walk around as they write, I see some who are able to put down the beginning and ending letters of words. It is my job to be ready to move them on to the next step when they will listen for other sounds in the words and put those letters down, too.

CONCLUSION

At this news-writing time, I show my students the special journal notebooks that they brought in at the start of the year with their supplies. *"These are your special journals,"* I tell them. *"Soon, you will get the chance to write some news in them every day."*

They can't wait to write in their journals and ask me about this often. Giving them something to look forward to is one more way of building students' enthusiasm and motivation.

Phase 2-4:
Letter-Sounds(2)
Alphabet Stories & Vowels

TWO KINDS OF ALPHABET STORIES

1. Class-Made Alphabet Stories
2. Reproducible Alphabet Stories

1: CLASS-MADE ALPHABET STORIES

Shortly after introducing the students to writing short stories, it is time to expand this process to include writing class alphabet stories.

Dd

Here is Dino.
He is a good dog.
He loves to dig.
Dino is a funny dog.

Figure 2-4-1
A typical class-made alphabet story composed on a chart with the class during Shared Writing, then run-off for each student to read and illustrate.

My goals for this activity are...

- to give students the added fun and challenge of composing stories that include words beginning with a specific letter.
- to give practice in using letter-sounds.
- to give practice in looking around the room to find the word they want to write but don't know how to spell.
- to show students how to check for staying on topic.
- to reinforce the story-writing skills they are learning.

Introducing the Composing of Alphabet Stories

1. I choose a letter, usually one of the two letters we are working with in our letter-sounds that week, and write the upper and lowercase forms of the letter (for this example: "M" "m") separately on the chalkboard with space for writing words underneath. Then I remind the students that we use uppercase letters to begin names of people and places and to start the first word in a sentence.

2. We make the "m" sound. I ask the class for names that begin with "M" and write those names under the "M" on the board (Maria, Michael, Marcus, and Michelle). *They also give me the names of places* (Miami and Mexico) and I write those as well.

3. Next, we look at the lowercase "m".
   "Make the "m" sound and keep saying it until you think of a word starting with that sound." After we get a few words on the lowercase list, I tell the students they can add to the list during the week.

4. One of the "m" words is "mouse", so the children decide to write a story about a mouse. They decide to name her Maria, a name listed under "M".

   "Where do I write the title of the story?" I ask, and they remind me to put it in the middle at the top of the chart page. I write the title, "Maria Mouse".

5.   *"Think of some sentences about the mouse. Remember, we want to have as many "m" words as we can in our story."*
They spot "move" and "monkey". *"You are so smart!"* I tell them. "Now I'm going to write the first sentence to get the story started."

6.   I say the sentence, *"Here is Maria Mouse,"* and write the word "Here". *"Who wants to spell 'is' for me?"* I ask knowing that most of them can spell this word.
      Someone volunteers, and I write "is" after "Here". *"Now I'm going to write Maria Mouse."* They spell the words for me from the title.

7.   *"Can somebody give me a sentence about the mouse that has the word "move" in it?"* I ask.
      "She moves to a new house," Olivia says.
      "What a smart girl! Some of those words are in our room. The first word we need is 'she'. Who can find 'she'?"

      Alex raises his hand. *"Point to the word and spell it for me while I write it,"* I tell him. We continue in this way through the rest of the sentence, and I encourage the students to look around the charts and words on the walls to find the words they want to write.

8.   *"Now for the last sentence. Who can make up a sentence about the mouse and the monkey?"*

      Troy waves his hand in excitement, "Her new friend is a monkey." is his sentence. We talk about the words in that sentence, and again I choose a few students to point the words out and spell them as I write.

> Maria Mouse
>
> Here is Maria Mouse.
>
> She moves to a new mouse hole.
>
> Her new friend is a monkey.

9. Last, we read the story through, checking that each sentence makes sense and is about Maria Mouse. Then we check that each sentence begins with an uppercase letter and ends with a period. Now we are ready to post the story chart on a wall.

We continue to write alphabet stories for several weeks to help students who are having difficulty with the letter sounds.

2. REPRODUCIBLE ALPHABET STORIES

There are several books or sets of reproducible alphabet stories. They are used by many teachers of kindergarten and first grade. The sets I use have a story for the teacher to read to the students and two pages of pictures with words. The students cut out the pages and put them together into little books.

These stories not only reinforce specific letter sounds, but they enable me to teach skills that will be needed soon when students begin to read books.

My main goals in using reproducible stories are…

- to improve the students' ability to hear and identify beginning letter-sounds.
- to develop their ability to recall information they have heard.
- to provide more opportunity for listening comprehension.
- to further encourage oral participation in class discussions.
- to give students practice in sequencing picture stories.

Steps in Using These Alphabet Stories

1. Copy the pages for each child. Make the book with them step by step for the first few times. (They trim the edges and cut each sheet into four pages.)

2. Together, sequence the pages from 1-8 and staple the books. It is important to take time with this and not try to rush everything into one sitting. Have them write their names on the books and set them aside for the next day.

3. Next day, gather the students into a circle with their books. Introduce the title and the letter-sound you will be working with.

   This is how I proceed:

4. *"I'm going to read you a story,"* I tell the students. *"You have your own little book that goes with the story. I will tell you when to turn to the next page."*
   "The title begins with the sound 'J'. I want you to listen for all the words that begin with the 'J'." Together, we think of words that begin with "J".

5. Slowly, I read the part of the story that goes with the first page. (The students' books do not have the story on each page, but they are looking at the pictures that go with the story.) Then I ask them, *"What words did you hear that begin with 'J'?"* Several students raise their hands and tell me the words. *"Great listening!"* I say. We make the "j" sound again to help the others listen for words.

6. I continue to read page by page, stopping at each page to ask for the words starting with "j".

7. Then, we go back and identify the pictures and words on each page. We discuss what happened in the story on that page, and I notice which students are able to recall the events. During the discussion, I ask questions to see how many students understand the story and the sequence.

Follow Up Activity

   Glue a copy of each picture page of the story onto felt for students to sequence and retell during Center Time.

After using these alphabet stories weekly for several weeks, I use them only occasionally, integrating them into general activities. I tell students the particular letter-sound ahead of time, so they can have fun guessing the name of the main character. Students love these alphabet storybooks and look forward to taking them home and retelling the story to their parents.

INTRODUCING VOWELS AND THEIR SOUNDS

"Today, this smart class is ready to learn about vowels," I tell the students as they sit on the mat in front of the chalkboard. *"There are five letters that are very special. They are called vowels. Watch as I write them on the board."*

They watch as I write the lowercase "a", "e", "i", "o", and "u" at the top of the board, and then say the letters with me several times.

"We meet these letters all the time," I tell them. *"They are in many words. Look around the room and see if you can find a word that has one of these five letters in it. If you do, raise your hand."* Quickly, all the hands go up.

"You all found words," I say. *"a, e, i, o, and u are busy letters, and they all have two sounds, a long sound and a short sound. In the next few weeks, you will learn the short vowel sounds."*

"Today you will learn the sound for the short 'a'," I tell the class. *"It says 'ah'. Say it with me. It is the sound the doctor tells you to make when he wants to look at your throat."* We make the 'ah' sound together.

"Now, say it again and keep saying it until you think of a word that starts with the 'ah' sound," I tell them. They tell me "apple', "at", "ant", "Alex", and "alligator", and I write these words under the 'a' on the board. We read the words together, listening for the 'ah' sound at the beginning, and then I ask them to think of a sentence for each word,

I write the sentences they give me on the chalkboard for the students to see. We read them together, and I leave them on the board for the rest of the week. We spend approximately a week learning and reinforcing each vowel. This includes working with the Word Families for that vowel.

Short Vowel Activities

There are many vowel activities you can use with the whole class. Some can also be part of the Reading Center. Here are a few activities you could use:

- For class practice I use magnetic consonant letters, adding them after the vowel and before it, pronouncing each vowel-consonant or consonant-vowel combination. These letters can be left on the board and used as a Reading Center activity.
- You can also use the three "Gathering Activities" in Phase 1-7 (page 76) substituting short vowel sounds instead of letters.

Looking at "Word Families"

A few days after introducing a short vowel, I begin to show students the "Word Families" for that vowel. For example, with the short "a" sound, I have the -at, -am, -an, -ap, and -ad families. The more families you use for each vowel, the sooner your students will grasp the concept and will be able to work with the individual vowel sounds.

This is how I introduce one word family, the "-am" Family.

I make a chart by writing "-am" six times, one underneath the other. Next, I prepare little letter cards for "p", "b", "h", "r", "y", and "s". I gather the children in a circle on the rug and review the short "a" sound. I point to the word ending "-am" and have them say it with me.

"In my family everyone has the same last name. It is the McLaughlin Family. Now we are going to talk about the "-am"

family." I label my chart "The 'am' Family" and explain to my students that all the words in this family will have "-am" at the end.

I place six consonant letters on the chalkboard. Then, I point to each letter and have the students say the sound. Next, they watch me model for them to show them what I want them to do.

I pick up the letter "h", make the sound, and say, *"'h' says 'h'."* (*the letter sound.*) *When I put it next to -am, it becomes 'ham'.*" Now it is the students' turn. I have a volunteer come up, choose a letter, say the sound, and place it in front of the '-am'. We continue until all the letters are gone.

The chart stays on the chalkboard near the Reading Center, so that the students can practice during the week.

For each vowel I follow the same procedure. There are many interesting and effective commercial phonics activities and also computer software that teachers use which are successful in teaching the vowel sounds. The best of these provide activities that link phonics learning to music, rhyme, and movement. Try to find these active, hands-on activities where a group of students or the whole class is learning together. They are much more fun and are more effective tools than the "Color, cut, and paste" worksheets.

I have seen many classrooms where students appear to be learning phonics by completing "fill in the blanks with the missing vowel" worksheets. These worksheets keep the students busy, but very often they have not grasped the concept. When you give lots of oral and hands-on practice in saying the sounds and writing them down, they will be able to use these skills in their reading and writing.

Soon, some of the students apply their short vowel skills in their own writing. I make sure there is no pressure on the students and try to keep the learning simple and fun. I know that first grade teachers will spend more time extending these skills to help reading and writing grow.

What about the long vowel sounds?

Once the students have learned and applied the short vowel sounds, the long vowels are so much easier for them to hear when they listen to words. They are, however, more complex with regard to spelling. Of course, some students have already encountered the long vowels informally when they read and write and when the class participates in a Shared Writing activity.

You will see how I introduce long vowels to the class in "Phase 3-1: Letter Sounds (3)".

CONCLUSION

In this chapter the students have moved from reading the sentences of a story written on a page, to following and retelling a story in an eight-page book. They have been introduced to vowel sounds. Also, they have reinforced their ability to listen for sounds in words when they are composing stories. In the next chapter you will see how the students expand their abilities to listen for sounds in words and use these and other skills to help their writing to grow.

The methods discussed in this chapter will help your students' writing grow in several ways. They include the following:

- Two ways to help students put their thoughts into writing:
    1. "Stretch and Write"
    2. Counting words in a sentence and writing them in sequence
- Learning to write more through sequencing.
- Learning to sequence through retelling stories.
- Spelling while writing.
- Journal writing

First, let's look at what the students are doing in writing.

After about two months in kindergarten, writing has become a bigger part of the students' day, and they love it.

- Most of the students are using words they know and words they see around them in the classroom to make sentences.

- A few are still drawing pictures and writing letters.

- A few are writing strings of letters, but are able to read back what they have written.

- They are writing and illustrating their own news stories and stories that they make up.

- Some are listening to the initial and ending letter-sounds to write the words they want to put in their stories but don't yet know how to spell.

- They are asking their classmates to spell words for them.

- They are practicing writing lists of the words they know how to spell on pieces of paper and on small chalkboards in the Reading and Writing Centers.

- They are putting spaces between their words.

- Some are putting periods everywhere.

> Early in kindergarten, most students write strings of random letters and words they know how to spell. But soon, a few students begin to take time to sound out the words they want to use. Because this takes longer than writing strings of random letters or writing the words they know, they will write less for a while. Their taking time to listen to the sounds in words as they write gives me a signal that they are ready to think more about the sentences and stories they write.
>
> I want to encourage these students to write more and to continue sounding out the words they want to write, so I provide more writing opportunities for them along with activities that will help them to sound out words.

TWO WAYS TO HELP STUDENTS
PUT THEIR THOUGHTS IN WRITING

Now that we have begun to write short stories and news, my goal is to encourage the students to write their thoughts in sentences, using the words they want to write and putting the words in order.

How do I do this? I teach the students two skills:

1. Stretching and writing words.
2. Counting words in a sentence and writing them in sequence.

1. "Stretch and Write"

Use words that your students are familiar with. The goal is to show them that words are made up of sounds. Take the word 'not', for example, and break the sounds down for them " n-o-t". Then do the same with some of the other sight words, stretching them to help the students listen to the sounds in these words. To give them more practice with this, I involve them in fun activities with the whole class participating.

ACTIVITY ONE: *"Find the Word"*

1. Write a few one-syllable words such as "bag", "man", "big", "dog", and "cat" on cards and post them randomly on the chalkboard.
2. Sound through a word, stretching the sounds.
3. The students look at the words and try to find the one being sounded out.
4. Select a student to come up and choose the sounded word.
5. Continue sounding through the words one at a time.

ACTIVITY TWO: *"Find the Letters and Make the Word"*

1. Place letters for up to five words randomly on the chalkboard.
2. The teacher stretches a word so the students can hear the sounds.
3. Students volunteer to come up, find the letters and make the word they heard.
4. They feel comfortable trying to form the word in front of the class, knowing that, if they run into difficulty, their classmates will help them out. When the word is made, we all give a silent cheer for the student.

ACTIVITY THREE: *"Write the Word"*

1. The teacher stretches a word and students volunteer to come up and write the word on the board.
2. Later on, when they are comfortable with doing this, the

students sit with individual chalkboards or paper to write each word as it is being stretched.

I spend quality time on these activities every day, and many of the students catch on very quickly. How can they pick up this skill so fast? I feel it is because they are having a hands-on experience with immediate positive feedback.

2. Counting Words in a Sentence & Writing Them in Sequence

Now that the students know how to stretch words and write them down, I move them right into sounding out and writing their own sentences.

- My first step in teaching this skill is to dictate a short sentence, for example: "My dad went to work".
- I hold my hand up and point to each finger as I slowly repeat the sentence.
- *"How many words?"* I ask them. We all agree there are five words.
- I write the words of the sentence on the board with the students helping to sound them out. Then I draw their attention to the spaces between words.
- When we finish writing the sentence, we check to make sure we have five words written down.
- After a few more examples, I have the students take over the writing.

> Every time I reach this stage in leading children into writing, I get excited because I know that, after using these techniques a few times, many students will take a great leap forward with their writing.

LEARNING TO "WRITE MORE" THROUGH SEQUENCING

A good way to help students develop sequencing in their writing is to model for them using Morning News and base the model on sequence. This is how I do it:

I begin by telling the class how I start the day. *"First, I get up. Then, I take a shower. Next, I brush my teeth and comb my hair. After that, I have breakfast. Last, I get in the car and drive to school."*

"It is the same way when you write your story, " I tell the class. *"You have to think, 'What happens first?' and write it down. Then you think 'What happens next?' and you write it down. And you keep doing that until you get to the end of the story."* I explain to them that if I just said, *"I got up and drove to school"*, I would have left out some of the things I did.

"That is what I did. Now, I want you to tell me what you did before you came to school today. Make sure you tell me what happened first, what happened next, and what happened last."

A few children come up to the front to tell their stories, and, boy, do we hear some long stories. That is fine. At this stage in kindergarten we want them to "tell more" in their stories. Once they are able to do this orally, they will begin to do it with their writing.

Next, I remind them of my story and write it on a chart with the students helping me to sound out the words. When we get to a word they know how to spell, I say, *"Do we know how to spell that?"* and they tell me the spelling right away. I remind them that they can find some of the words around the room. The next time I model writing in sequence, I use a student's oral story.

When they all sit down to write their own stories about how they start the day, I tell them to begin from when they first get up in the morning and write until they get to school. As they write, I walk around, helping them to think and add more. Soon, they begin to catch on to the idea.

LEARNING TO SEQUENCE
THROUGH RETELLING STORIES

The skill of retelling stories is very important in kindergarten. When children are able to verbalize and organize their thoughts, they become better writers. Once they try to sound out their words and writing begins to flow, structure becomes important. Thinking about sequence as they write is the first step in learning how to structure their writing.

The students already have had some experience with retelling stories. When we prepared to dramatize nursery rhymes during the first few weeks, we always went over the sequence of events first. Also during Story-Reading Time, I encouraged the students to orally retell simpler versions of the stories some of them already knew, like *Goldilocks and the Three Bears*, *The Three Little Pigs*, and *The Gingerbread Boy*. Now it is time to choose a story for them to retell in writing.

The Steps of Introducing
the Retelling of a Story in Writing

1. It is important to choose the story wisely. You will need a simple story with very little dialogue in it. Summarize as you go along when reading a story for the class to retell in writing, leaving out parts that are not important. This makes the story easier for these young children to retell. A long, complex story will confuse them when they begin to rewrite.

2. After reading the story, have one or two students come up and do a short oral summary before the children go back to their seats to start writing. Then remind the class of the main sequence they should include in their stories.

3. When they begin to write, some students will be apprehensive because this is new for them. It is your job to move around,

building up their confidence and helping them get started. This skill should be a pressure-free activity. It will be a skill they use over and over again, so limit the time they spend on it at the start, and gradually increase time as they become more comfortable. Tell them, *"It is okay if you don't finish your story now. I will help you finish it later."*

4.   At first only a few students at a time take off with the skill of retelling in writing. Not every child is ready to grasp this skill. A few are writing strings of letters and can read back what they have written, so they have the oral retelling skill. Some students write two or three sentences and stop. They have the ideas in their heads, but they are not yet at the maturity level where they can keep on writing. As the music plays and you walk around, look for these students and stop with them for a few minutes to help them think about what else to write.

Encourage your students and help them to write more. *"Look at how much you have written! Please read it to me,"* I say. After they read, I tell them, *"Wow! You have done a great job. What else happened in the story?"* Slowly, we review the sequence together to help them write more. This seems to be just what they need to enable them to continue writing.

"Look at your page. It's almost full!" I exclaim when I next see them. *"I have more paper if you need it. That's what good writers do. They keep adding until they have more pages."*

When children learn in an atmosphere where it is safe to take risks, they will try to sound out the words they want to write as soon as they have the skills to do this, and that is when writing begins to flow. The more independent these writers become, the more time I get to spend with students who are

writing less and need more help in adding to the story and
putting the sounds down.

Fig. 4-2-1: (left) In
this first page of her
retelling of a pumpkin
story, the student wrote
the words she wanted to
use, sounding through any
words she didn't know and
couldn't find in the
charts, sentences, and
words around the room.

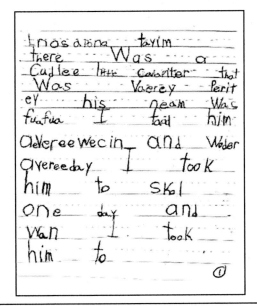

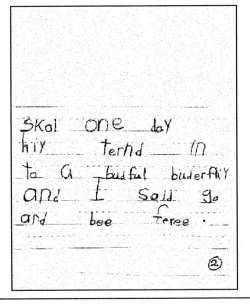

Fig. 4-2-3: (above) This student's Writing Center story
reads: *"Once upon a time there was a cuddly little
caterpillar that was very pretty. His name was Fuafua.
I fed him every week and water every day. I took him to
school one day and when I took him to school one day he
turned into a beautiful butterfly and I said go and be
free."*

LISTING WORDS THEY KNOW HOW TO SPELL

Continue to give students practice in writing the words they know how to spell.

This activity starts soon after the beginning of the school year and continues throughout the year. You will have heard me mention it before. Here is one way to do it.

1. Hand out sheets of paper folded into eight squares and tell the class, *"On this sheet of paper write as many words as you know how to spell. These words are already in your brain. When you finish writing them, you will stand up and read your words. It doesn't matter if you just know a few words because you will be learning to write more."*

2. Before passing out the paper, I model how to do this. *"Let me show you how many words I can write without looking around the room."* They sit on the rug as I put one of the sheets on the chalkboard and write. I fill up my squares with the students watching me. When I have finished, I say to the students, *"Did I look round the room?"*

   "No," comes the response.

   "You see boys and girls, you already have a lot of words in your brains that you know how to write."

3. Everyone is anxious to go back to the tables and write the words. After passing out the sheets, I walk around to see the words they are writing. I am always amazed to find how many words they can spell... words that I never thought they would be able to write.

   "You are so smart. Soon you will fill both sides of your paper and get another sheet," I tell them.

Sure enough, they rise to the challenge. After a few weeks of doing this, they fill up the backs of their papers and many ask for a second sheet. Soon they will fill up a sixteen-space sheet. This is an important activity that will improve your students' writing and reading.

The	Your	Fish	Fun
to	There	house	Rain
make	Soft	dog	Six
They	Fat	Food	my
look	mat	am	OFF
you	box	BAHAMAS	one

Some	Jonna	So	He
Fox	Sun	a	and
Fishing	into	Fzzy	not
See	Let	teeth	all
BEd	go	Eat	oh
mom	Seen	milk	FrEE

Fig. 4-2-3

A student's list of words

> Every time they write, remind your students that they already have some words in their brains. *"Don't wait if you know the word. Write it down and move on to the ones you don't know. This helps you write faster."*

JOURNAL WRITING

After a month or so of the students writing their news and thoughts on sheets of paper (See Phase 2-3), I bring out the notebooks they brought in with their supplies at the start of the year. They have been waiting for this and are excited.

Before handing out the notebooks, I tell them, *"This is a very special book. It is called your journal. You will write special stories in it about things you do at home, things we do in school, and trips we go on. You will also write about places you go to over the weekend and on holidays."*

"First, you must write the date at the top of the page every time you write in your journal," I tell them. I show them my journal and model how to write the date at the top of the first page, where to begin to write, and how to write all the way across to the edge of the page.

Although these spiral notebook pages are lined, I do not tell the students to write on the lines. I don't want to pressure them to do this before they are ready, so we have not talked about writing on lines yet. It is interesting to note that the informal training I do in Phase 1-5, when I show them how to write their sight word sentences on the creases of a sheet folded in four horizontally, seems to influence students. Now that they have their journals, everyone makes an effort to write on the lines. My emphasis goes into training them to fill up each line by starting each sentence on the left and writing to the end of the line.

Figure 2-5-2:

An example of an early journal entry. You can see how the student is trying to sound out the words he wants to use.

From this time on, the students write in their journals on a regular basis, and they see me write in mine. I spend time helping each student think of what he or she would like to write. At sharing time, we share what we have written. When I share my own journal, they see that they can write about everything they did or just write about one thing. They write anywhere from one or two sentences to a whole page.

Some students copy down words and sentences they see around the room, but most of them try to listen for sounds in the words they want to write. It doesn't matter what their skill level is or how they get their stories down, as long as they know what they meant to write. Soon the whole class knows that, when it is Journal Time, *everybody* writes.

Fig. 2-5-5: When students first begin to write their stories, a few will write using sight words posted around the room. This student can tell you the story he wanted to write, but, at the moment, he is not yet at the stage of writing the words that make up his story.

Two months later the same student is sounding out words to tell his story.

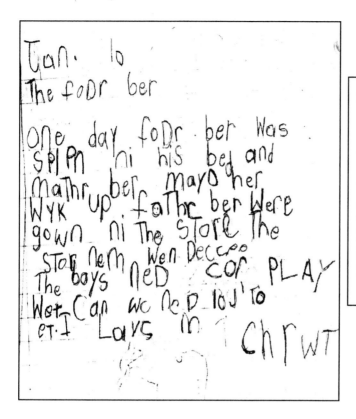

Fig. 2-5-6: You can see how the same student is now listening to the sounds of the words that tell his story and writing the words down as best he can. When this happens, writing begins to flow.

Once students are able to flow with writing, they take a great step forward. Turn the page to see what an advanced student can produce in her journal by the end of January after just a few months of reading and writing.

Fig. 2-5-7: (Story on next page)

You can see much from this top-group student's journal story: She is doing an excellent job of "sounding out" the spellings of words she does not know. She is flowing with writing. She has absorbed storytelling patterns from her reading and listening to stories and is using them in her own stories. Can you tell that she loves to write?

January 22, 2001
once upon a time there
was a little girl and
a cat and she was sad.
but she asked her mom
if she cad go in the
patting zoo and she taled
her mom city was gone
avre she thoth her citin
was gone and she Began
to criy her citin was only
hiding Be cas she was goin
to have four little citins
I can't find a citin so she
went Bac home for dinner but
when they got at the house.
the little girl went in her
room maybe she is hiding
from me she looked. all
arownd the house she looked
in the cichin she looked in
the bathroom she look in the
clozit she looked ander the
liveing room chare she looked in
mommys room and she
looked in daddys room and the
veurey laste Aayse she
looked ondr her bed. the end

CONCLUSION

Now that your students are becoming more able to write down the words and sentences they want to write, and now that they are thinking of sequencing and asking "What happened next?" when they write their stories, you will notice that their stories become longer. You will also find that their excitement in writing grows as they take pride in the stories they write.

REMEMBER...

- Accept whatever your students write with pleasure and excitement.

- Have them share what they write with the class.

- Display their work proudly in the classroom.

Phase Three

"Expanding Reading and Writing"

The chapters in Phase Three cover what happens in literacy learning during the second half of the year.

```
┌─────────────────────────────────────────────┐
│            ┌───────────────────┐             │
│            │  Phase 3-1:       │             │
│            ├───────────────────┤             │
│            │ Letter Sounds(3)  │             │
│            └───────────────────┘             │
│                                              │
└─────────────────────────────────────────────┘
```

In this chapter we will discuss how to teach more letter-sounds and other decoding skills to the kindergarten students who show they are ready. They will learn about the following:

- Consonant blends
- Digraphs
- Long vowel sounds.
- Compound words

Some of these skills might seem too complex for five-year-olds, yet, when they are ready, children learn them without difficulty. How can this happen?

The secret is that they are having fun, and they learn the skills through the natural flow of their work. They are not working through drills and worksheets. They don't have to sit down and work with sounds and words over and over. They grasp the skills easily and naturally, like they learn to talk. When you give examples of how we use these sounds and words everyday, the children realize how much they already use them in their daily conversations. Then they see what the sounds and words look like in writing, and they make the connection.

CONSONANT BLENDS

When do I begin to teach consonant blends?

By the time five or six weeks of the school year have passed, a number of students have learned the letter sounds so quickly that they are sounding out words in their writing. Some of the words they want to write begin with consonant blends, so I start teaching about blends with the individual students who are ready.

This informal teaching happens when I model writing for the class, during writing conferences, and during group reading. Students come across words with blends naturally as they read and write. Words like "friend", "play", "store", and "clothes" are among the first "blend" words that kindergarten students want to use. It would be both unwise and unfair to expect these students to wait several more months to learn about blends until the rest of the class is ready.

Once you find students who are using words with blends, teach them the blends they need. Just stop and take the time to point out the two sounds that make the blend they want to use, give them examples of other words that begin with the same blend, and get them to give you examples. Continue to reinforce the concept of blends informally during reading and writing.

Now that students are beginning to read books and sound out the words they want in writing, it is time for a fun activity to introduce consonant blends to the whole class.

Introducing Blends to the Class

Activity One: *"Joining Together"*

Choose a blend, for example "pl". Hold up the "p" letter card and choose a child to be called "p", taping the letter on her chest so that the class can see. Choose another child to be called the "l" sound, and tape the letter on his chest. The whole class says the two separate sounds. Then you can tell a story. *"First "p" was playing by herself. Then "l" came over. Now they are playing together so we are going to give them one name "pl".* The class makes the blend sound "pl".

Repeat the process with the same students or new students several times to practice blending the two sounds into one. Then do the same with a few other blends, choosing them at random.

Once the students have participated in this hands-on activity a few times and they understand the concept, I use the letter cards on my chalkboard, and we separate and put together blends as further practice.

Activity Two: *"Saying the Blend"*

For another class activity, post the letters on the board, say the two letters, and select a student to come up. The student finds those letters, holds them up, makes the two sounds separately, and then holds them together and makes the sound of the blend.

Activity Three: *"Finding Blend Words"*

- Post six blends on separate brightly-colored cards across the board. The students make the sound as you place each blend on the board.
- Tell the class they are going to find words for each blend. Then choose a blend at random. Ask the class to give you some samples of words for that blend and write them underneath.
- Do the same with all the blends, making sure you have at least five words written for each.

Activity Four: *"Say the Blend & Find a Word"*

Keep your "blend" cards handy, and at any time of the day, pause to hand out blends to students. They should make the sound for their blend and say a word for it.

After all the students with cards have had their turn, they pass them to another classmate and the activity continues.

Activity Five: *"Write the Blend"*

Make a blend sound and have the class join in and make the sound with you. Then choose a volunteer student to write the blend letters on the board. For the purpose of helping writing, always say some words with each blend.

> Learning phonics is an essential component in learning to read and write, but if every practice is a drill, students can experience difficulty and feel pressure to learn. When using fun activities, make sure there is no pressure to perform and assist any student who is not sure of the skill.

DIGRAPHS

"WH" WORDS

Early in the year, I expose the children informally to the "WH" (blowing) sound by showing them the "Question Word" cards: "when", "where", "what", "which" and "why" as I ask comprehension questions about the stories I read to them (Phase 1-6). I also add "who" so that I can point out that the "wh" in this word is pronounced differently. When I ask a comprehension question about the stories I read to them or stories they read in their groups, I hold up the appropriate question word card. By doing this, they can't help but learn to recognize the words. Even when they are reading books in groups, I use the same techniques.

Now I talk more formally about the "wh" sound. Together we make the "blowing sound, and they give me words that start with this sound. I write the words the students give me on the board: white, wheel, whisper, whale, whistle, whip, etc. Reading over the words and sounding through them seems to be all it takes to help students remember this sound.

"TH" WORDS

One of the first sight words the students learn after they start the year is the word "the". When they are able to recognize it in text, I show them that, if I put different letters on the end, we get new words. They learn to recognize "then", "them" and "they" and find these words everywhere in text.

I say the two "th" sounds and tell them that whenever they see a word starting with "th" they should put their tongue between their teeth. We practice with "the", "then", and "them" by adding and removing the "n" and the "m" to the word "the". Later we tackle "there" and "that", and I teach the class to look at the end of these words to differentiate between them.

We make a list of words that start with the other "th" sound: think, thing, thunder, thank-you, and read them together.

Easing Confusion with "th" and "wh" Words

Many children are confused by the four and five letter "th" and "wh" words. You can prevent this if you expose them to these words early and in a fun way.

An activity that has been successful for me over the years is to have students role-play Mom and Dad asking "wh" questions such as "Where are you?"; "What are you doing?"; "Who opened the door?", and "Why don't you go to bed?". Children can also role-play "Teacher Talk". Have them use the question word cards when they play the game.

Students quickly learn to identify difficult words when you use catchy little techniques. For example with "wh" words such as "who" and "why", after I use the words in sentences, I show the students that "who" has an "o" at the end and "why" has a "y" at the end. We then discuss examples of how they hear "who" and "why" used at home.

Follow Up Activity

1. Place the "th" or "wh" flashcard words on the chalkboard.
2. Have the children name the words together.
3. Choose a child to pick up a word, name the word, and use it in a sentence.
4. Write a few of the sentences on the chalkboard, so that the children can see them in writing.
5. Later on, place the "th" and "wh" word cards in the Writing Center, so that the children can use them there.

"SH" AND "CH"

1. I introduce the "sh" and "ch" separately. We have fun making the "Be Quiet" sound or the "Sneeze" sound. Then they give me words that begin with each digraph, and I write them on the board under the "sh" or "ch" heading. Next, of course, they put the words into sentences.

149

2. In another "sh" or "ch" activity, I say a word and select a student, who repeats the word and then writes on the chalkboard the digraph he or she has heard at the beginning or end of the word. Soon these digraphs will start showing up in the students' story and journal writing. As children learn skills, they need to apply them, and that should be done through their reading and writing.

When students become comfortable with the blends and digraphs at the beginning of words, provide activities where they have the opportunity to sound through words that have these sounds in the middle and at the end. It can be as simple as writing words on the board for the class to sound through. When you spend time doing this, you will notice how quickly your students apply what they have learned.

LONG VOWEL SOUNDS

How wonderful it is to know that these five-year-olds are already reading when they come to learn about long vowels! Instead of being drilled in consonant and vowel sounds as a way to begin reading, they can already read many sight words, sentences, and stories on charts, and most are reading books.

Remember that this is not the first time some of the students have been exposed to the long vowel sounds. I have informally talked about these sounds with individual students as they meet long vowel words in their reading and writing. Also, I mentioned them when they began to learn the short vowel sounds. Now, it is time to have a whole class activity to identify the long vowel sounds, to help students hear the difference between the long and short vowel sounds, and to help them recognize the long vowel sounds in words.

I remind the students that each vowel has two sounds, and we begin with an activity using the two sounds for the vowel "a". Before introducing this activity, I review the short vowel sounds and a few of the Word Families they have learned. Some Word Families are posted on charts round the room.

"Sort Those Vowels"

1.   *"Today, you will begin learning about long vowels. Let's look at the 'a'. It has a long sound and a short sound. You already know the short sound."* We make the short sound for the 'a' together.

    "Listen to the long 'a' sound … Watch my mouth… 'ay' Now you say it." They all say the sound.

    "Do you notice anything?" I ask them. Some students notice that the long sound is the same as saying the letter. *"You are so smart,"* I tell them.

2. I write "short a" and "long a" on separate cards. Then I divide the class into two: the 'long a' section and the 'short a' section. I tell them, *"When I hold up the long 'a', whoever is on that side of the room will say 'ay' and when I hold up the short 'a' card, whoever is on the short a side will say 'ah'."* We practice and then switch sections.

3. *"Now, I will put some word cards on the board. Some will have the long 'a' sound and some will have the short 'a' sound."*

    I place the following word cards on the board: made, rat, face, cap. tape, cat, pale, sat, hat, came, plate, shape, rap, and ham.

4. Next, I choose a volunteer to come up and pick a word. The student names the word. *"Listen for the two 'a' sounds again. The short 'a' says 'ah'. The long 'a' says 'ay'. Now watch my mouth when I say the word 'tape'. Which sound do you hear?"* They tell me they hear the long "a" sound. Then I say, *"Yes, 'tape' has the long 'a' sound so I put it under the long 'a' on the board."*

5. *"Now, it is your turn to try. You will pick up a word. Say it, and place it under the correct card on the board."*

    They take turns until all the word cards are in place.

> When I work with the long and short
> sounds of a vowel together, it becomes
> easier for the students to differentiate
> between the two sounds. I encourage you
> to be creative and to make these phonics
> activities as enjoyable as possible.

I continue this activity as I introduce the other long vowel sounds. Some of the spellings of long vowels can become complex, so I stay with the a-e spelling to keep this learning fun. I reinforce the learning of long vowels through long vowel word families like: "-ake", "-ate", "-ace", etc. As the students become more experienced readers and writers, they will find it easier to apply the phonics skills they have learned.

COMPOUND WORDS

Soon after the beginning of the year, we bump into compound words. They appear in our poems and stories and in the sight words the children are learning. We stop to look at them. I show the students how they can cover up one part of the word to find what the other word says. Then we put the parts together. *"Whenever you find a word like this made up of two little words, it is called a compound word."* I tell them.

After being introduced to the concept, the children often point out words they think are compound words when they come across them. We stop to check that there are two little words in the word they have found and then make the decision as to whether or not it is a compound word.

Follow-Up Activities

- To reinforce their learning and have fun with compound words, I write as many simple compound words as I can find on cards:

sandbox, backpack, into, today, playground, myself, outside, anytime, everywhere, everyone, everybody, someone, somewhere, etc. Next, I cut them into the separate words. Each student gets one part of a compound word. Then we play the "Match-Up" game, in which they move around the room. When I signal them to stop, they have to find the person with the other part of their compound word.

• We also play "Match-Up" using a pocket chart in the reading center where they can sort and combine the word parts into compound words. I add compound words to my "Sight Word Sheet" where the students toss the beanbag and say the words.

The words in themselves are simple to understand. Once we discuss their meanings and students use them in sentences, they never forget them. When I read stories, they stop me to tell me I just said a compound word.

CONCLUSION

Children will catch on to the skills needed to work with blends, digraphs, long vowels, and the compound words at their own pace, but by exposing them to these sounds and words, you speed up the learning process. When you add meaning to the words by putting them in sentences, the children also learn faster.

By the time these students tackle the more complex skills of phonics during their First Grade year, they will already have developed a love for reading and have gained confidence in their ability to learn.

Remember

Limit the number of worksheets you use to reinforce phonics skills or cut them out entirely. Have the children practice the letter-sounds through fun oral activities and through using them in the context of their reading and writing.

Phase 3-2:
Moving Forward with Reading

In Phase 3 we are discussing what happens during the last half of the year. By this half-way point, all except a few students are reading books in small groups. They are increasing their ability to sound out new words and are adding daily to their reading vocabulary. Your main job as teacher is to spot when they are ready for the next step and to move them on. This chapter includes the following sections:

1. Knowing where your students are in reading
2. The teacher's role with each group
3. More about working with themes
4. Encouraging and expanding independent reading

Fig. 3-2-1: Students in a reading group work cooperatively, independent of the teacher, to sound out new words, read through the book, and talk about the story.

KNOWING WHERE YOUR STUDENTS ARE IN READING

> Being aware of where my students are in learning to read, monitoring the steps they take, and knowing when it is time to move them to the next level, all enable me to help young children make the most progress.

How could I know when a group of students is ready for a more advanced text if I didn't spend time with the group, listening to them read and checking for comprehension? The answer is that I couldn't.

At the time of writing this chapter, I have seven reading groups in my class of thirty students. Most students in this class are ESOL/ESL and many are economically disadvantaged. Yet, by working in small groups at their own level, they have made good progress.

By now, all but one group of four students can receive a new set of books, and, without my help, can cooperatively work through the process of discovering the story and reading the book (with the possible exception of one or two words that are hard to decode). They are able to do this, because, right from the first time they read a book in a group, I have modeled what to do and trained them to do this by themselves. This training of the groups to work cooperatively, independent of adult supervision is what gives me the opportunity to be with each group one at a time.

THE TEACHER'S ROLE WITH EACH GROUP

When I go to a group where the students have had a new book for a couple of days, they will often tell me that they already know all the words in that book. By trying as a group to sound through the new words and by using context and picture clues, they have decoded the words successfully and have already read through the book. After I come to sit with them, this is what we do:

1. We talk about the characters, where the story takes place, and what happens in the story itself.

2. *"Did you come across any new words that were difficult to understand?"* I ask next. I use these new words in different sentences to help them grasp the meaning. Then, I ask them to find the words in context on certain pages in the book.

3. After that, it is time for a variety of comprehension questions: some factual and some higher level inference and "What if" questions.

4. The last thing we do with that book is to sit together while each student takes a turn to read a page. The students know that this is the procedure we follow before they move on to the next group book.

5. Now that the group has finished with that book, I bring new "reading table" books down from the shelf and let the students each choose a book to read independently for their own enjoyment. This is something they love to do and look forward to. It provides a good incentive for them to finish reading the group book.

MORE ABOUT WORKING WITH THEMES

As I explained in Phase One, I use themes to enhance literacy skills throughout the year. Through theme activities, students have had many opportunities to experience reading and writing in creative ways with art, crafts, music, and movement. At this time of the year, the themes serve as an ideal way of supplementing the group reading of books with activities where they read to learn about the theme topics.

All through the year, the walls of my classroom have been covered with poems and information charts about the current class theme for students to read during whole group lessons and at Center Time. At this time of the year, I am able to increase the number of sentences on the theme information charts and to use more difficult vocabulary words. The students can now read the poems and some of the books I provide about the theme topics. They can also write their own imaginary stories and copy pictures of the animals or insects from the charts.

Fig. 3-2-2:

A student reads a poem about a caterpillar aloud during a class lesson on a "Bugs" theme. Above her head is an information chart.

At this time of the year, I also include another type of chart on which the students read information and use vocabulary word cards to fill in the blanks in the text. It is important that the information charts are written legibly and with text that most of the children can read.

When a chart is first introduced, we read it aloud together and discuss the information. Later, during Center Time, the students can choose to read these charts independently or with their partners.

ENCOURAGING AND EXPANDING INDEPENDENT READING

This is the time of year to encourage and expand independent reading for students who are ready. Remind the students that they may read independently when they finish their classwork and during Center Time. They may choose what they want to read: charts, books on the book table, poems, magazines, books they borrow from the school media center, stories displayed on the walls that other students have written, etc. Students also enjoy sharing a book with others who are not in their reading group.

Figure 3-2-3:

Two students read books of their choice to each other at the Reading Table.

Checking Out Classroom Books

No matter how many books a student has access to outside school, it is always a joy for them to be able to take home the books they read in school. They enjoy reading them aloud to their family and neighbors. One student even took them to read to his Sunday school class.

When you allow students to take books home, make sure they understand the importance of taking care of the books: of putting them back in their plastic bags, zipping the bags, and returning them. My students quickly get to know that if they lose the books, they will not be able to check out others for a while.

Student Check-Out

Students can do the paperwork themselves. As soon as group reading of books begins, each student gets a sheet of paper and puts his or her name on it. Every time students check out a book, they write the title of the book and the author's name on their sheet of paper. When they return the book, I check it off to show that the book has been returned. This sheet also serves as part of the record of books they read during the year.

Fun Reading Time

By March, I begin "Fun Reading Time" close to the end of certain days. I divide the class into four mixed ability groups. Every student chooses a book that they would like to read to the group. The rule is that they all take turns to read two to four pages of the book they chose.

Each group gets into a circle with one student acting as facilitator. They call on the students in their group one at a time to read from their books to the group. At this time all the patient training I did with the class at the start of the year and reinforced throughout the year really pays off. My students are able to work cooperatively. I do not need to be there listening to them, because the children know what they have to do and quickly get into a routine where they do not need supervision.

Moving Along with Reading Skills

As soon as I see they are ready, I encourage students to change from using their fingers to keep the place, to keeping place with their eyes. I also train them to read silently "like your Mom and Dad".

Expanding Independent Reading

Figure 3-2-4:

Silently and independently, a student reads a book she has chosen from the Reading Table and quickly becomes engrossed.

During the final two months, I give the students more opportunities to choose their own books. They may read with a partner, read in a small group, or read alone. Many of them choose to read alone, especially those mature students who are reading "just with their eyes". A few of the top students are now reading books from early series "Chapter" books like the "Junie B. Jones" books and the "Arthur" Chapter books. They find a little corner and get lost in their books. They lead the way by their example, and soon others, too, are reading independently and silently.

Reading takes place during Group Reading Time, as part of class themes, and during Center Time. Whatever reading the students do, I check to make sure that they are not only reading but that comprehension is taking place.

Adding Games That Involve Reading

At this time of year, I introduce games that involve reading (like Junior Trivia) for the students to play independently in their groups. All these games need is reinforcement of turn-taking skills as well as initial training in reading the questions and in giving the group enough time to think up the answers.

CONCLUSION

Before long, reading becomes automatic for the children. It happens all through the curriculum and all day, because most activities they do involve reading, whether reading directions in the math book and on theme work sheets or reading the student weekly newspaper.

> Reading continues in this way until the end of the school year, with small groups working at their own pace and the skills in this chapter being introduced when the teacher sees the students are ready.

Phase 3-3:
Moving Forward With Writing

In this chapter we will look at what you can do to move your students forward with writing during the second half of the year. It will include the following:

- Helping students who are still taking "tiny steps" with writing. (Other "tiny step" students are now making bigger steps and are already on their way.)
- More ways to improve spelling.
- Helping writing to continue growing.

1. HELPING STUDENTS WHO ARE STILL TAKING "TINY STEPS" IN WRITING

Writing is as important as reading. In writing, as in reading, students show signs of readiness at different times. By early spring or before, most of the students I teach are comfortable with writing and sounding out the words they want to write. This is the time when others become ready to move ahead: students who had a late start or perhaps no pre-school experience or ESOL/ESL students whose English language was not yet developed at the beginning of the year.

Let's look at what these students who are still taking "tiny steps" are doing in writing.

- Their thoughts are flowing as they write.

- They are filling up their pages with words, because they have come to realize that words make up a story.

163

- When they read to you what they have written, they will tell you a whole story, but what you see is not that story. Most times they are writing sentences that are from the sentence strips or words they are familiar with. They know that stories are told in words, but they have not yet begun to try to write the actual words of their stories on paper.

> Composing orally is the first step in learning to compose in writing. To require students to sound out the words they want to use before they are ready, only turns them off writing. They shut down and no longer want to try because they begin to compare themselves with faster classmates. By now, however, these "tiny step" students are usually ready.

The Boost into Writing

1. Every time I see students beginning to make the connection between sounds and letters, I know they are ready for a boost into writing. I gather a small group of these students at the chalkboard and reinforce their phonemic blending skills so that they will learn how to sound through the words they want to write. I dictate a sentence to them, and we slowly work through the sentence, sounding out one word at a time while they take turns to write the words on the board.

   This writing at the chalkboard with a small group of "tiny step" students and going through the process of stretching the words, listening for the sounds, and writing the letters... and doing it time after time, is what makes the breakthrough possible.

2. After working with the group, I spend a few minutes with each of these students at the Writing Center and also when the class is writing journals, to encourage them to apply

this "sounding out" skill in their writing. I also write stories on chart paper with them to give more practice.

Being part of a small group of students, all of them at the same learning level, frees "tiny step" students from feeling intimidated by faster writers. They gain the confidence to begin the necessary trial and error period as they venture into sounding out the words they want to write.

Remember

- You have to show the same excitement when you receive the work of these "tiny step" students as you do with the work of students who write well. Show that you enjoy the stories they have in their minds, because they put a lot of thought into what they would like to write.

- Practice of the phonics skills they are acquiring should occur through the students using the skills during meaningful writing activities instead of through the use of skill worksheets. That way, they will not be at a loss as to how to apply phonics in real writing situations.

- And once again, because it is so important, I remind you to give *all* students the freedom to write and to love writing, before expecting them to sound through the words they want to write.

---

2.   MORE WAYS TO IMPROVE SPELLING

- Helping spelling skills to grow
- Bringing rhythm into spelling words
- Keeping up the challenge

Helping Spelling Skills to Grow

1. From the start of the year, the students have spoken aloud the letters of every new sight word that they learned to read on flash cards, sentence strips, or wall charts. At first this regular saying of letters reinforced letter recognition. Now, it has a second pay-off in their ability to write some of these words correctly from memory.

   Continue reminding your students that there are many words they already know and are able to spell. Do it before they begin class writing and before Center Time. Remind them that some words are made up of two little words and are easier to write.

2. Show them how to add "ing" and "ed" to words.

3. The students are definitely becoming much more aware of the spellings of words they write. They have done so much reading by the second half of the year that they remember what the words they write should "look like". To encourage this, I sometimes point to a word they have written (for example "wet" for "went") and say, *"Look at this word again."* and they will quickly say, "Oh, I left out the 'n'."

   Gradually, as they build their skills during the year, your students' spellings will become more correct. Remember that, if you pressure them to spell correctly and you notice their spelling errors in a negative way, they will stop using sounded words and limit themselves to the "safe" words they know how to spell.

Bringing Rhythm into Spelling Words

Children should feel that spelling and writing are fun. Using rhythm to help them learn to spell common words is one way of adding fun to learning.

By this time of the year, some students are ready to work in cooperative groups to memorize words they want to use in writing. On a sheet of paper, I list a few commonly used words that are often spelled incorrectly in their writing. Then I show them what to do. We gather in a group, say each word, and then repeat the letters to a rhythmic clapping. Students can be as creative as they want with the clapping rhythms. They can also slap their knees or snap their fingers. Different children can lead. They can do the rhythmic spelling in teams moving to the rhythms. Soon I challenge these students to see how many of them can write the words from the list when I say them. By adding rhythm, spellings are learned, and spelling becomes fun.

Once other students see this rhythmic spelling being done, they want to be a part of this activity, too. I let them try with two or three words and watch carefully. If they are ready, they are free to participate in this spelling activity but with fewer, simpler words. If I see they are not ready, I do not pressure them. I want learning to read and write to be a joyful experience.

Another reason for dictating words for students to write is that I want to introduce them to the way spellings are learned in First Grade. From this time to the end of the year, I choose common words that they encounter in their writing and reading and give them five words a week to practice learning on their own. If they choose to take the words home, they can. However, they have a few minutes during Reading Time every day to work together on learning the spellings. There is no pressure. Eventually and gradually these words turn up in their stories correctly spelled. This rhythmic spelling activity will provide benefits for both reading and writing.

Keeping up the Challenge

Once students have finished learning the spelling words, I keep the pace going because I know that many of the students in the top groups are ready for this next step. I want them to

learn how to write sentences around the spelling words. As part
of this activity, I want them to put each sentence on a new line
and number it, and I want them to be sure to start with a capital
letter and end with a punctuation mark.

I'm So happy.
What did You say ?
I'm Come ing.
Jack and Jill Went up a hill.
You Are Walk ing.
I see You Play ing.

Fig. 3-3-1: (above left) A student writes a list of
spelling words from dictation.

Fig. 3-3-2: (above right) The same student writes
sentences around the spelling words. A teacher
conference will help to show her how to join the
"ing" onto the words and how to number each one as
she goes.

At this point I introduce the top group to the three
different kinds of written sentences. (Earlier in the year, they
already composed different kinds of sentences orally with sight
words.) I write examples so that they can see how the same word
can be used in a sentence that ends with a question mark, an
exclamation mark, or a period. I remind them always to make sure
each sentence begins with a different word.

Ex: I like to go shopping.
Will you go with me?
Ready, set, go!

In the same way that I watch for groups in reading that are ready to move to a more difficult text, I also look for the next set of students ready to take this more advanced step in spelling without being pressured. It is this ability on the part of the teacher to move groups forward when they are ready that keeps the excitement and energy for learning in high gear.

> Moving forward should be happening in all your groups in all subjects. As soon as you teach a skill to one group, look around for the next students who will be ready for that skill.

3. HELPING WRITING TO CONTINUE GROWING

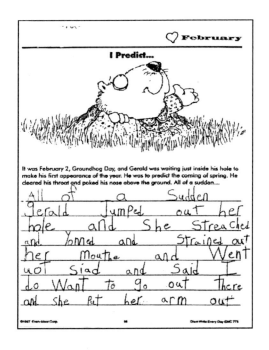

and Said it's Colde So
She Went back in her
hole.

Fig. 3-3-3: A top group student has no trouble finishing a Groundhog Day story start. She has already read many books and is flowing with writing. She is using sounding out and visual memory to spell the words she does not know.

By this time of the year, students often get ideas for stories from the information they are learning in the current theme, from the fictional books we read, and from the field trips we take. They are expanding their stories to many pages, and I am encouraging them to stay with the topic.

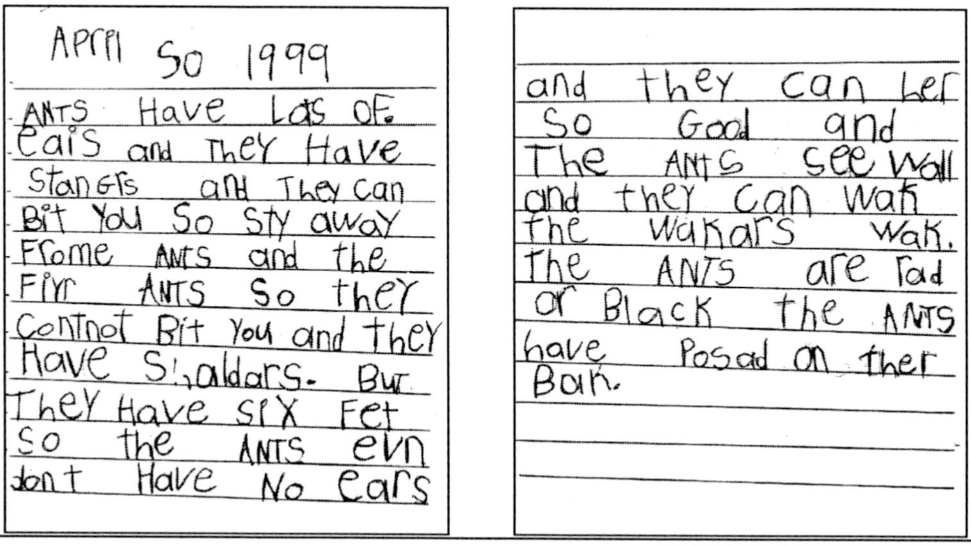

APrrl So 1999
ANTS Have Los OF.
ears and They Have
stangrs and They can
Bit You So Sty away
Frome ANTS and the
Fir ANTS So they
Contnot Bit you and they
Have Shaldars. Bur
They Have SiX Fet
So the ANTS evn
dont Have No ears

and they can Ler
So Good and
The ANTS See Wall
and they can wak
the Wakars wak.
The ANTS are Tad
or Black the ANTS
have Posad on ther
Bai.

Fig. 3-3-4: A two-page account that a student wrote about what he has learned about ants. This was composed when the class wrote about insects during an April "Bugs" theme. This student is able to write down his thoughts and sound out any word he wants to spell.

Taking Writing Home to Finish

Once they write more and their stories become longer, students often find that they have not finished their stories when Writing Time is over for the day. They want to continue writing and are not satisfied until they have the entire story written down. They often ask, "May I take my story home and finish it?" or "May I finish it tomorrow?"

Never overlook how wonderful it is for kindergarten students to love writing so much that they want to continue with their stories. This excitement with writing needs to be encouraged. If you encourage children to flow with writing and give them positive feedback, their passion for writing will grow.

1

The moster in The closit

One day a boy
Was gowan to
Gat drast and
He hrd a
roooo! Com! hir!
com! hir no
I Wilnot go

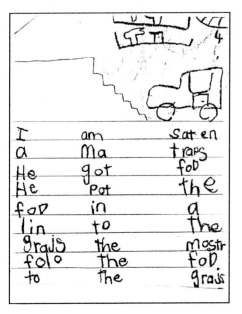

2

Momy Ther is
a moster in
my Closit Ther
iS no Soh
thig as monrit
wot is in
my closit I
am Comen up
Ther See har

3

is nofig in
your closit But
mommy har is
a moster in
my Closit if
You Pot Stop
Tocen adot mosts
I wiln not
Toc to you

4

I am sat en
a Ma traps
He got fob
He pot the
fob in a
lin to the
grais the mostr
folo the fob
to the grais

Fig. 3-3-5: A student retells a story he has read. He
writes quickly, sounding out at least half of the words
he wants to use and getting close enough that you can
tell what words he wanted to write. A reminder about
word space will help him overcome the "column" writing.

I find that parents are excited to see their children's progress in writing, however, you need to prepare the parents when writing is going home. You see, almost always, when students take their stories home to finish, the parents want to sit with the child to make sure that every word is spelled correctly. When a parent (or teacher) begins to spell words for the student to make sure they are all correct, the child loses confidence and will not trust his or her own judgment any more. With emergent writers, this stops the creative flow of the story and slows the growth of their writing skills.

The best way to handle this is to talk to the parents or to send a note home to ask them not to correct spelling and to suggest ways in which they can positively support their child during this emergent writing stage. I let them know that, at this stage in kindergarten, my main focus is to get the children to write and to have their thoughts flow. After I communicate with them, parents understand and realize that the correct spelling will come as their children mature and become more experienced writers.

A "WRITE AND SHARE" ACTIVITY

- Take a group of students who are writing at the same level. Sit them in a circle. Provide each student and yourself with a clipboard, a   sheet of paper, and pencil.

- Tell your students, _"We're going to have a fun writing activity."_ This is how I introduce it. _"I will say a word and then you write a sentence using that word. After that, I will read my sentence to you and give you a chance to write your own sentence."_

- I say a word, for example, "happy". Then, I write a sentence, "The children are happy." I show it to my students and say, _"It is your turn to give me a sentence using the word "happy"._

- They orally give me their sentences, and I tell them, _"Now, write your sentence on the clipboard paper."_

- After they have written their sentences, the children share what they wrote.

- We follow the same pattern for the next sentence.
- After I tell them the next word, we all write our sentences at the same time. I encourage the students not to begin each sentence with "I".   Then we share what we have written.

This activity takes away the fear of writing, because, after doing it a few times, I find that the children become able to keep their focus on their own writing.   They feel comfortable because they are working at the same level and they know they will get their sentences finished in time.   Also they become more comfortable with spelling the words they want to put down.   You will find that, after doing this activity a few times, their story writing will flow better.

Reinforcing Some Writing Conventions

As well as encouraging more writing, my goals for the last quarter of the year are to continue reinforcing the conventions of writing that the students have been learning through the year. Before every writing activity, I say to my students, *"Remember that it is very important to start with a capital letter and put an ending punctuation mark after the last word of your sentence. Also, always make sure you put a finger space between each word so that others can read what you write."*

At this time of the year, some students are beginning to understand the use of the capital letter and the period in sentences.   Before they write, I model writing a few short sentences and show them how I pause, put a period and think for a moment about what I will write next.   *"Now, I have another sentence to write, so I have to begin with a capital letter,"* I tell them.

At the Kindergarten level this is a slow process, but it helps them to get ready for First Grade.   They may not put the period in every time, but by modeling this sequence over and over again, I find that they gradually begin to understand.

Learning to Focus Deeply When Writing

All teachers have their preferences for the kind of atmosphere their students write in. I have found that students focus better when music is playing and they are able to get into their thoughts without being interrupted. Thus, early in the year, I create a quiet, focused environment by playing peaceful music during class writing time.

When the students are in the Writing Center, however, they have the freedom to write about whatever they wish. They are free to discuss their work and talk about spelling with the other students. I encourage the more mature writers who want to be alone with their thoughts to move into a quiet place by themselves when they are composing. It is a joy to see that, even at this young age, some students are already developing the ability to go inside themselves when they write.

The Freedom to Write

Giving your kindergarten students the freedom to write without fear of having what is wrong pointed out to them, enables them to develop a love for writing and confidence in themselves as writers.

CONCLUSION

Be accepting of the writing your students produce at whatever stage of writing they are, and show your excitement at what they achieve. Watch for the steps forward that will happen and be ready to support that learning. Remember that having a risk-free atmosphere in your classroom will enable your emerging writers to experiment and grow.

Phase 3-4: Winding Up the Year

As the year draws to a close, paperwork increases and end-of-year assessment has to be done. This is the time when we look very closely at each student.

END-OF-YEAR ASSESSMENT

All through the year, I have used the school district assessment tools for reading. These tools include the following segments:

Concepts of Print
Letter Recognition
Beginning Sounds
Word Recognition
Phonemic Blending
Phonemic Segmentation
Reading Running Records

Now, at the end of the year, I verify what I already know. The students have made great gains. A few are reading at an end of second grade level. Some are reading at an early to middle second grade level, some are reading at a middle to end of first grade level, and a few are reading at an end of kindergarten level. This happens every year.

I do not give a formal assessment for writing at the end of kindergarten, however, by keeping samples of their writing in a portfolio throughout the year, it is easy to see what the students have achieved. They have come from scribble writing or drawing and writing a few words, to flowing with writing.

Using the methods in this book, I find that, year after year, most of my students finish kindergarten able to sound out the words they want to write and put their thoughts down on paper. Most are able to "flow" with writing and spell many of the common words correctly. They can write their news, make up imaginary stories, retell stories, and write about theme topics. They are beginning to use capitals and punctuation. They have experienced a joyful and successful kindergarten year.

Every year my students' academic success brings me great satisfaction. But more than anything else, it is the joy they experience while becoming readers and writers that I am most proud of. I hope this early success and joy in learning will enable them to soar to ever-greater heights.

CELEBRATING THE LEARNING

It is important to celebrate the learning that has taken place during the year. In this positive model of teaching, we celebrate the progress students make every day and cheer on the steps taken by individual students, however, now it is time to celebrate the whole year.

> Try celebrating the year of learning with your students' parents at a special Parents' Night or Parents' Lunch. The parents will be as proud and thrilled as you are with the progress their children have made.

I always take the time at the end of the year to sit with the class and help them to become aware of the learning and changes that have taken place inside them during the year and of the scope of the journey they have made in kindergarten.

I help them do this by talking to them as a class and leading them back over the year. We have fun remembering what they were like when they came through the door all those months ago. They remember again how they felt, how many of them did not know their letters, and how they even had to learn to line up and come to sit in the front. They laugh when they remember how much they did not know. We remember the many special things we did together: the trips we went on and the special school events that we took part in, and their faces show astonishment at how much we have done.

I pass out to them their individual sheets of paper with the lists of books they have read during the year, and they are amazed at how many books are listed on their sheets. They look through the portfolios of their writing and art and can see how far they have come. At the end of this discussion, after all the remembering is over, I encourage them to write a letter to me about their experience in kindergarten and how they feel now that the year is ending. Then we all share the thoughts we have written.

Figs. 5-3-1:

End-of-year letters are a good way to help students wind up the year and say, "Goodbye" to their kindergarten experience.

After the memories and letters are over, we talk about the summer vacation and about how wonderful it will be for them to be in First Grade when summer is over.

The final day of the school year arrives, bringing both joy and sadness as the children leave kindergarten for the last time. Every year, as I watch them leave for the summer, I find myself wishing I could go with them into First Grade. Then I stop and remember the twenty-five to thirty new kindergarten students who will come into my classroom in August, and I think, "If I took this class this far, just imagine what I could do with next year's kindergarten."

My wish for my students is that they will have a First Grade teacher who will continue their successful journey. I hope their teacher will first assess them to see where they are at the end of the summer and then will keep their motivation high by challenging them to keep moving to higher-level skills. Because so many of them are working above grade level, I worry that, if they are made to repeat skills they have already learned, some may become bored, lose their motivation, and become behavior problems. These young children can't express themselves and ask to be challenged, so it will be up to their teachers. My hopes for their continued success go with them as they leave.

Concluding Thoughts

The school year comes to an end, and it is time to wind down from the high spirits and positive energy that have carried me through the year. I think of the students who now leave my classroom as readers and writers with an excellent foundation of skills, and I feel excited and fulfilled at the results. We have worked cooperatively and joyfully together and have accomplished much.

Their success once again reinforces my belief that all students can learn. Parents are often amazed at how quickly very young children learn to walk and talk. Some children also flow quickly into reading and writing. Unfortunately, this does not happen for all. Children learn differently, and, as teachers, we have to use a variety of techniques so that every child can learn what we teach.

Children cannot change the environment into which they are born. They cannot change the fact that they were not read to during their first five years or that they were not provided with early opportunities for language to develop. They should not be prejudged as to their learning potential and looked on with lower expectations for what they cannot change. Those early disadvantages may mean that these children take "tiny steps" in learning at the beginning, but those disadvantages do not stop them from learning.

In many other parts of the world, brilliant students and great leaders are produced where most homes never had a book for parents to read to their children. Often the language in schools and books may be different from the language they speak at home. These children may write on slates with chalk or even in the dirt with sticks as they begin to learn to read and write. Most of them are not blessed with materials even the poorest of our students take for granted, and yet they manage to learn to read and write.

Every year, in spite of having more resources to use and six years of teaching, some of our young children leave elementary school without being able to read and write well enough to handle the learning needs of Middle School. Except in certain cases, these children have the intelligence and ability to learn, so we must conclude that the methods we are using with them need to be changed and the expectations of the school, home, and community should be raised.

We teachers are the ones who must make the learning happen in our classroom. We are the motivators. If, in only a few weeks, kindergarten students from all backgrounds can learn to recognize the letters of the alphabet and many sight words, how much more are they capable of learning in a year? What all young students need is to have teachers who believe in their ability to learn and who organize their teaching so that students learn to read and write through meaningful reading and writing.

A good learning program must provide the opportunity for every child to progress successfully through the reading and writing steps at his or her own pace. Just as children move sequentially through the stages of development, they also need to move through sequential stages of learning to read and write. The only way for them to do this at their own pace is for children to learn and work in small groups at the level where they can succeed.

> It is very important for every child
> entering kindergarten to experience
> early success with learning.

In this book, you have found the principles and methods that have worked so successfully for me over many years of teaching kindergarten and which are now working well for other teachers of emergent and early readers and writers. I am sure that, as you implement these methods in your classroom and become more and more comfortable with this literacy model, you too, will achieve the same or greater success, and I wish you good luck in your future endeavors.

POSTSCRIPT

Since writing the earlier part of this book, I have had the opportunity to put the McLaughlin Model Pilot Program (the program using the methods I have set down in this book) into effect in several schools in Palm Beach County, Florida. We are finishing the second year of the pilot program, and it continues to grow and be highly successful.

Mentoring these pilot teachers has shown me that this program can work for all teachers. They are achieving the same success that I achieved year after year with my kindergarten students. They have documented their success, and are very excited at the results. They are looking forward to helping train other teachers in this model during the Summer Training Sessions. Next year, the Pilot Program will continue to have a strong and positive impact on the success of students and teachers taking part.

Josephine McLaughlin
May 2003

┌─────────────────────────────────┐
│   Appendix A: │
│   A Look at Three Students   │
│   │
└─────────────────────────────────┘

"J"

A student I will call "J" emigrated from a country in Africa and entered my class in January. She spoke no English and did not understand what I said to her. Her father could speak English and was able to communicate with me. "J" was a very friendly child and was eager to learn.

As she had no experience with the English language, I had to take her back to the first steps and work one-on-one with her to help her learn the letters of the alphabet. My assistant, Mrs. Covington, also worked diligently with her. Along with learning the letters, I had "J" work on sight words starting with naming and action words, which she associated with objects in the classroom, actions, and pictures. In only two to three weeks, "J" was able to identify the letters of the alphabet and an impressive list of sight words.

Soon I moved her into building and reading sentences around the sight words she knew and also using these words to build simple stories. "J" felt so secure working with my assistant, her classmates, and me that she caught on very quickly. Within a month, we were seeing rapid acquisition of new words and basic sentence structure. She was learning the English language through reading and hearing the language around her.

"J" was eager to begin reading books so that she could be like the others in the class. I let her join the group that was closest to her level so that she could observe how they pointed at the words and followed along with the story. Then I introduced her to her first book. I knew that it would take a while for her to be able to comprehend what the words meant, so I spent some time pointing to the pictures and naming what was there. Then, I guided her into reading the book.

Although her understanding of English was very limited, her English vocabulary increased rapidly. Before long, she could read the book, understanding what the sentences were saying. I let her take that first book home, so that her family could share in her excitement. They were amazed and asked how she had learned to read that quickly. Along with the book she took home, I gave her a list of the new words she had encountered in her book and in poems that we read, so that she could practice them at home. These were words that I knew she would encounter in the books that would follow.

She was now reading and was able to move quickly into another group. This rate of progress surprised all of us. I feel that much of her fast progress was due to the excitement she saw in the students around her when they finished a book and knew they would move on to the next. She got caught up in their excitement for learning.

When she was experiencing success in learning, it was time to introduce her to the sounds. She joined the group of students who were still learning the sounds of the letters. Like the other ESOL students, her spoken English improved to where she was able to express herself in discussions and communicate with the other students. She could orally answer comprehension questions about the stories I read aloud to the class, but it took some time for her to be able to express herself in writing.

By the end of the school year, she was able to blend sounds together to make a word. She was reading almost at the "end of first grade" level, and she could write several sentences. She still needed me to sit with her to put her thoughts into writing and to stay with a topic. Left on her own, she would write sentences with familiar words that did not pertain to the topic. I knew that once she had a little more experience with the English language, she would become a top student.

"M"

"M" joined the class in mid December. He came from a regular kindergarten class in another school in the county. My first impression was that he was an intelligent child. He was highly verbal and eager to participate in discussions. However, I was surprised that he could only recognize some of the letters of the alphabet and no sight words at a time when 80% of my class was reading books. From observing him, I knew that I must challenge this child or he would slip into having behavior problems.

"M" told me that he couldn't read words like my students could. *"Don't worry. I'll teach you,"* I told him. With the help of his classmates, he took off. He was very eager to catch up. It was as though he was in a race. Watching his classmates read and write motivated him. He wanted to be just as good at reading and writing as they were. When I saw how excited he was, I placed him with a reading group and kept close watch on how he was doing. As soon as he mastered that book, I moved him to the next group. The more success he achieved, the more motivated he became. In a matter of a few months, he surpassed many of his classmates.

I gave him no time to get bored. Many times I pulled him aside to let him read to me or to introduce him to a more advanced text that would prepare him to join a higher group. He learned the letter-sounds with the other students, and I gave him the freedom to write and feel comfortable with writing before I laid any more expectations on him. Then, one day, when I saw that he was ready, I sat down with him and helped him to write a story about what he did at the weekend. As he dictated his story, he slowly wrote one word at a time sounding out the words and writing them down. Amazingly, it took only one or two more occasions like that and this child mastered the ability to write anything he wanted with sounded spelling. Not only was he writing and spelling better, but he also wrote on and on. He wanted to show that he could write two pages.

By the end of the year, "M" was reading at second grade level. He had come a long way in just five months.

"C"

"C" was in kindergarten from the start of the school year. At first he was very quiet, but later he opened up and began to participate in discussions. I noticed that he had good fine motor skills. However, when the groups began to learn the letters of the alphabet and the sight words, his progress was very slow. He was easily distracted, so instead of learning the letters from the big chart, I had to introduce him to two or three letters at a time to help him succeed. At the same time, he was learning sight words more easily but still taking longer than the other children.

Soon, "C" was able to read the four-sentence stories, but he still was not making much progress with the letters. He was taught by his peers, by my assistant, and he was taught by me, yet there was little progress.

After exhausting every method I could think of to improve his letter recognition, I decided to try a new approach. I taught him to remember the letters by practicing spelling the words in the stories he read. I told him that I would soon teach him to read a book, and as he learned to read it, I would let him take the book home and have his brother help him. Before this, "C" would not settle down to let his brother help him, but once he got the book, his behavior at home really improved. Finally, later in the year, "C" could find any word I named in a story he had read and spell it without hesitation.

By taking tiny steps "C" made steady progress, and by the end of the year he had met the requirements for progression to first grade.

It is especially important that students who learn with "tiny steps" get careful attention from their first grade teachers, so that the progress and the success they have achieved can continue.

Appendix B:
More Writing Samples

JOURNAL WRITING

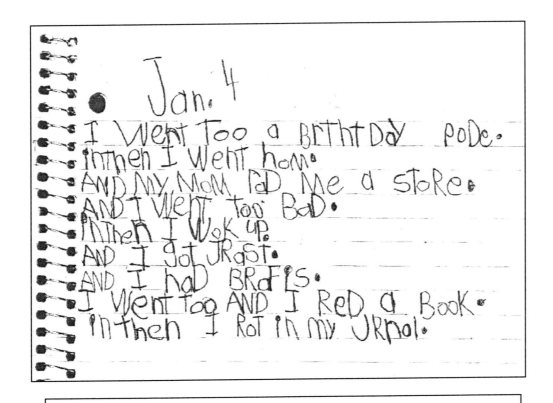

Fig. Appendix B-1:

This is an early journal entry. You can see how the student is using sounded words and words he knows how to spell. He is also doing a good job of narrating a sequence of events from going to a birthday party to writing his journal in school the next morning. He is already putting a period at the end of each thought. He has learned much about writing in just a few months.

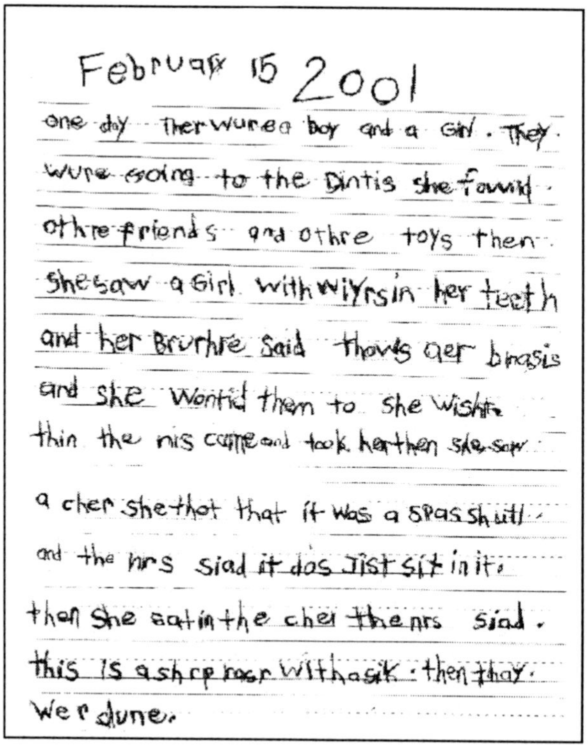

February 15 2001

one day ther wure a boy and a girl. They
wure going to the Dintis she found
othre friends and othre toys then
she saw a girl with wiyrsin her teeth
and her Brurhre said thows aer brasis
and she wontid them to she wishte
thin the nrs came and took her then she saw

a cher she thot that it was a spasshuttl
and the nrs siad it das jist sit in it
then she sat in the cher the nrs siad
this is a shrp roor with a sik then thay
wer dune.

Fig. B-2: When writing is flowing, students will usually write faster, sounding out words as quickly as they can so that they can tell the story that is flowing in their minds. It is important at this stage to affirm what they are doing right. Notice how this student has told a story with a beginning, middle and end. She is writing across the whole line and putting even spacing between her words. She is not afraid to tackle whatever word she wants to use. She is even putting some periods in correctly.

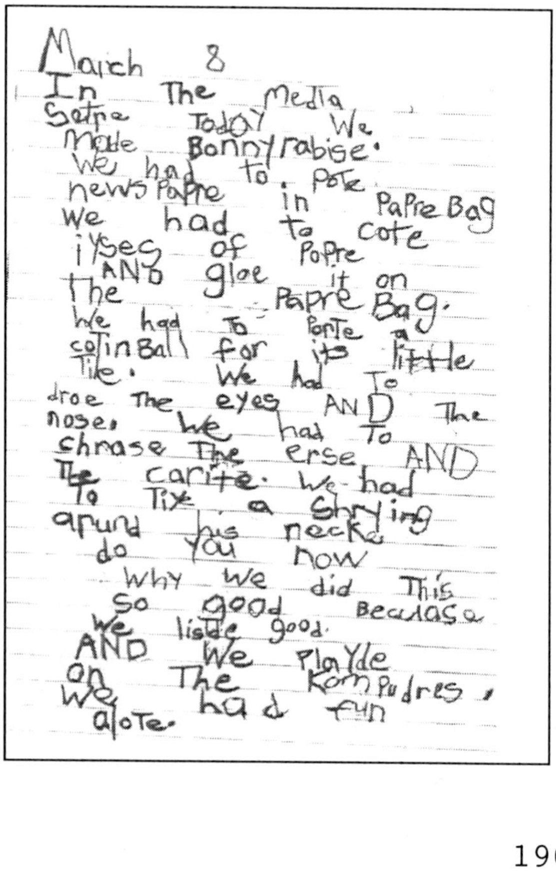

March 8
In The Media
Satre today we
made Bonny rabise.
We had to pote
newspapre in papre Bag
We had to cote
iysec of poptre
And gloe it on
the papre Bag.
We had to ponte a
cotin Ball for its little
tile. We had To
droe the eyes AND the
nose. We had to
shrase The erse AND
The carite. We had
to tixe a shrying
arund his neck
do you now
why we did this
so good becalasa
We lisde good.
AND We playde
on The komputdres,
We had fun
a lote.

Fig. B-3:

At journal time, I want students to flow with writing, so I do not talk to them about neatness or forming letters carefully. That is for handwriting practice and when neatness is important for display reasons. I am delighted that this student can tell how he made the bunny rabbit in the media center and that he sounded out the words he wanted to use.

WRITING CENTER STORIES

Just a mess

One Day I Plad Bass Ball and I lost
My Boll and I went To tall Mom
and I Said Mom Do you Kowe whrer
My Ball is and Mom said I Can, Thriy and
we lookD in My room anDit whas
a vary Yary Mesi So I cliD it up
and it Whsa clin and I Said thre
and I Said at last I Foued My Ball
and I Went to tall Mom and
She Saib good For you and then I
Went to Play Bass Ball

Fig. Appendix B-4 (Above):   Halfway through the year,
this student has learned to flow with writing.   Like
many other emergent writers, he is telling a story
linking the sentences with "and".

RETELLING STORIES

May 29, 2001
There was a happy shool
of fish that live in
the corner of the sea. there was
a bunch of red fish, but there was
one he on was black.
his name was swimmy. swimmy
swim faster then his
brothers and sisters and there
was this big thing behind us
it ate us accept for swimmy
he was fast. he went deeper
and deeper. he was sad. then

fish he said come on fish
they said no. we'v got to
do something. he did that
and that. I'v got it so
he showd them how to
form a fish. he was
The eye and they
scard the big thing that
was behind them.

Fig. Appendix B-5: This retelling is done by a top
group student. He has retold a story from memory
and in sequence. He shows an understanding of story
structure and for using periods at the end of
sentences.

191

E.S.O.L. (ESL) WRITING

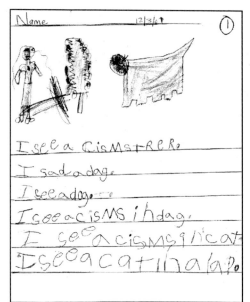

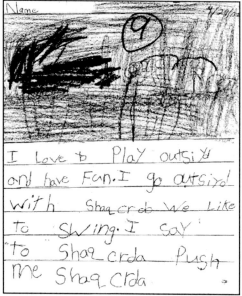

Fig. Appendix B-(6-9):

All three stories on this page were written by the same ESOL student, who came into the class in September not speaking any English.

By December (top left) the student is making up sentences using words she sees around the room and is starting to sound out other words.

By April (top right) she is writing sentences that make sense and sounding out her words.

By May (bottom left) she is also using mostly correct punctuation in her sentences.

Look at the boys and girls.
They like to play.
They run and jump.

We like school.
It is fun.
We can see our friends.

Here is my family.
This is my mother.
This is my father.
Here are my sister and brother.

It is fall.
Look at the beautiful leaves.
They are red, brown, yellow, and orange.

There are pumpkins on the vine.
Some are big.
Some are little.
Do you like them?

Long ago the Pilgrims sailed to America.
They came on a big ship called the Mayflower.
They were met by the Indians.

The Indians live in a tepee.
They go hunting and fishing.
Some Indians work on the farm.

Light the Menorah
one candle at a time.
Soon all eight candles will be burning.

     Christmas is coming.
     We will put lights on the tree.
     It will look so pretty.

Let's get ready for Kwanza.
Wear your pretty clothes.
You may choose red, yellow, green, or black.
We will eat and dance and sing.

     Winter in Florida is fun.
     Sometimes it gets cold,
      but there is no snow.
     We can still go to the beach.

The firefighters are our friends.
They come in a big, red, fire truck.
They will put out the fire.

     We use our senses every day
      in many different ways.
     Just think what our world would be like
      without things to touch, taste, see,
      hear, and smell.

In spring it gets warmer.
New leaves come on trees.
Soon birds will build nests and lay eggs.

About the Authors

Josephine McLaughlin

Josephine McLaughlin was born in Manchester, Jamaica, West Indies. In 1983, she graduated from Coppin State College, Baltimore, Maryland, with a bachelor's degree in Early Childhood Education. Since then she has taught kindergarten in schools in Palm Beach County, Florida. She received her Master's degree in Early Childhood Education from Nova Southeastern University in 2000. Her extraordinary success, year after year, in teaching young students of all different backgrounds to read and write brought many educators and the media to her classroom.

In 2001, the Palm Beach County school superintendent took Josephine out of the classroom to set up and implement the McLaughlin Model Pilot Program in several Title One schools in the district. This program has produced outstanding results, and is now being expanded to other schools. When she is not guiding the teachers in her Pilot Program, Josephine has fun singing and teaching her four-year-old granddaughter, Gabrielle, to read and write.

Sylvia Andrews

Sylvia Andrews grew up in a village in County Down, Northern Ireland. After she became a certified teacher, she taught elementary grades for several years in Ireland and the Bahamas. In 1976 she came to live in West Palm Beach, Florida, where she taught creative writing and reading in a private school. At present she teaches students with physical disabilities in Grades K – 12 with Palm Beach County School District. She is a graduate of Stranmillis Teachers College, Belfast, N. Ireland, and Florida Atlantic University, Boca Raton, Florida.

Sylvia is also an author. She has two picture books published by HarperCollins (*Rattlebone Rock* and *Dancing in my Bones*) and several poems published in anthologies by Meadowbrook Press. While giving in-service writing workshops for teachers, she met Josephine McLaughlin and became interested in her model of teaching emergent literacy. Sylvia organizes and chairs three writers' groups and is a member of the Society of Children's Book Writers and Illustrators.

ISBN 141200409-8